Praise for *More Time Ins, Not More Time Outs*

More Time Ins, Not More Time Outs, is one of the most insightful and transformative parenting guides I have read. It gently compels us to take ownership of the role we play in our children's misbehavior and provides practical tools and easy-to-follow roadmaps for cultivating self-awareness and parenting in a more reflective and compassionate way; in a way that truly honors the boundless love we have for our children (even on their worst day). Best of all, this book teaches parents the importance of being as tender, forgiving and empathetic with themselves as they strive to be with their children. A truly invigorating read.

— PETAL MODESTE
  Associate Dean of Student Affairs Administration at Columbia Law School & Mother to two amazing girls, ages 11 and 2!

One light is very bright, especially when it's dark. **This work is one heck of a bright light.** Dr. Becker has given us a beautifully written and most needed gift. Dr. Becker makes it possible for us to look at interchanges with our children and see how our actions can elicit the very behaviors that parents find most challenging in their children. She shines a forgiving light on our hidden feelings and histories so that, as parents, we can be more open to ourselves, better understand and gain control over personal threats to our vulnerabilities, improve our relationships with our children, and impact the behavior that prompted the seeking of help. Dr. Becker gives many wonderful examples so that knowing what to do and say becomes easier. She moves us from feeling hopeless to hopeful.

>—Dr. Beatrice Harris
>> Founder, Harris, Rothenberg International, Inc. Director, Human Behavior Change, Associate Well-Being, Humana, Inc.

More Time Ins, Not More Time Outs, is **much more than a primer** to understand the complex relationships between children and their parents. Having known Dr. Becker both professionally and personally for many years, I continue to be impressed by her non-judgmental work with families. The book is a must-read to understand how parents shape the behavior of their children. I celebrate her as an agent of everlasting hope and change.

>—Maria Vandor Danziger
>> Former Associate Commissioner
>> NYC Administration for Children's Services

As neither a parent nor an educator, I was not sure how much I'd benefit from reading *More Time Ins, Not More Time Outs* but I was mistaken. After reading, I became aware of the bullies that I know or have known (parents, bosses, and teachers) and can now better understand and reconcile their effect. As a board member of a not-for-profit agency that serves troubled youth, I can see the potential for a changing dialogue about responses to bullying and the long-term impact on behaviors.

>—Barbara K. Schoor
>> Board member and Officer
>> Collier Youth Services, a non-profit organizatin

This book will enhance your parenting skills. Its strategies can help you go from being your child's adversary to becoming her respected guide.

   —Janet Roen, M.D.
      Clinical Professor Emerita of Ophthalmology,
      Icahn Mt. Sinai School of Medicine.

You write with the same "voice" that you speak with: vernacular, funny, wry, serious, etc. It is an easy-entry read.

   I didn't think I'd be as interested in the subject as I became as I got into it; it resonates with some of my own behavior patterns and those of some of my friends; children/parents are your subject, but the lessons are more universally valuable.

   —Stephen Buchman
      Ombuds/Attorney Advisor/Of Counsel
      Norton Rose Fulbright US LLP
      Associate Director of Career Advising/
      Columbia Law School

More TIME INs, Not More TIME OUTs

PARENT WITHOUT BULLYING

A New Approach to Raising Children

Jaqueline H. Becker, Ph.D.

CWI, Inc.

Copyright © 2017 by Jaqueline H. Becker, Ph.D.

All rights reserved. No part of this book shall be reproduced or transmitted in any form or by any means, electronic, mechanical, magnetic, photographic including photocopying, recording or by any information storage and retrieval system, without prior written permission of the publisher. No patent liability is assumed with respect to the use of the information contained herein. Although every precaution has been taken in the preparation of this book, the publisher and author assume no responsibility for errors or omissions. Neither is any liability assumed for damages resulting from the use of the information contained herein.

Every effort has been made to obtain necessary permissions with reference to copyright material, both illustrative and quoted. We apologize for any omissions in this respect and will be pleased to make appropriate acknowledgements in any future edition.

ISBN 978-0-578-41181-1 Paperback

Library of Congress Control Number: 2017914171

Publisher:
CWI, Inc.
307 East 44th Street, Suite F
New York, NY 10017
Phone (212) 682-7600
www.communicationwithintention.com
cwidrb@gmail.com

Cover and interior design by Design for Books

Printed in USA

Disclaimer

Any resemblance to real people in this work is completely accidental. The examples are composites of everyone I have experienced.

Only connect! That was the whole of her sermon. Only connect the prose and the passion, and both will be exalted, and human love will be seen at its height. Live in fragments no longer. Only connect, and the beast and the monk, robbed of the isolation that is life to either, will die.

—E.M. Forster, *Howard's End*, 1910

For those who did,

For those who tried,

For those who couldn't and some who wouldn't,

You are my teachers, and I am eternally grateful to each of you.

—Jaqueline

Contents

Foreword ~ ix

Preface ~ xi

Note to Parents ~ xiii

Introduction ~ 1

1. Parent Without Bullying ~ 5

2. Bully Parenting in Action ~ 49

3. An Eight-Step Parenting Method ~ 65

4. Cyberbullying Help ~ 95

5. Time In: A New Parenting Tool ~ 119

6. The Power of Forgiving ~ 141

Helpful Resources ~ 145

Acknowledgments ~ 157

About the Author ~ 159

Foreword

There are words of praise for this work from colleagues who have letters after their names. I value their support and I know it's what publishers love to see. But I can think of no greater Foreword for this work than the appreciation from parents who, along with their children, have been set on a new and happier course for daily living. A few samples (names are changed):

> Dear Dr. Becker,
>
> I am so grateful for your work with Jeffrey and me. Focusing on more Time Ins with him has made a huge difference in my getting to know him better! I now am able to love his sensitive nature as opposed to be constantly resenting it. Time I didn't think I had, I found. And love I knew I felt, I found a way to give better.
>
> My heart-felt thanks,
> Alice

> Dear Dr. Becker,
>
> I love that you have helped Sarah be Sarah while she fixed her hideous behaviors.
>
> Love,
> David

Dear Dr. B.,

I know you told us his getting better is not a miracle; it's our hard work. But, truly, it still feels like a miracle.

Our sincere thanks,

Allison and Tammy

Preface

If I can stop one heart from breaking
I shall not live in vain;
If I can ease one life the aching,
Or cool the pain,
Or help one fainting robin
Unto his nest again,
I shall not live in vain.

—Emily Dickinson (1830–1886)

In this era of tumult, you will need to hold fast to that which anchors you to what is precious, good, and divine in yourself and in others.

More than ever, as the negativities that have lain dormant in our country (world) rise, your children will need you to be as aware of yourself as you can possibly be about how you parent them. Be assured that our abrasive and harassing era will pass just as other historically cruel, oppressive eras have passed. They are the necessary fodder for ushering in a new level of consciousness for our human development.

Because of *your efforts* to parent your *particular child* with more conscious awareness, you will become part of the weight that tips our scales from a conquering, bullying society to a more consciously compassionate one.

This book will add to your ***Bi-Conscious**** toolbox as you endeavor to parent more steadily, with less guilt and with more confidence, as you become more profoundly present with your child while fostering her growth. I know you want to.

> Dr. Jaqueline H. Becker
> NY & CT

***Bi-Consciousness** (term invented by Dr. Becker) is the awareness that you are driven to act by unconscious, as well as conscious, components of your personality.*

Note To Parents Regarding You And Bullying

Who doesn't bully? We all do, in singular moments and/or in patterns. That is why I am calling bullying a *spectrum disorder*. And yes, a disorder, since I do not think most of us would intentionally bully anyone, and especially not her own child, unless *something* is disordered in her ability to control her unkind behaviors in a moment, or pattern of moments.

A definition of bulling is, "[To] use superior strength or influence to intimidate (someone), typically, to force him or her to do what one wants." I mean, really, what parent hasn't done that? So don't worry and think that if you "bully" your child from time to time you are, thus, "a bully parent." Not at all, just a human.

Spectrum is defined as, "[it is] used to classify something, or suggest that it can be classified, in terms of its position on a scale between two extreme or opposite points."

Let's look at the syndrome Attention Deficit Hyperactivity Disorder (ADHD), which as with other syndromes, has certain symptoms that form clusters. One such cluster of type for ADHD is inattention. Within that cluster we find the symptom of *difficulty paying attention*. As part of a meaningful ADHD diagnosis, we cannot just look at that symptom, period, and end of story. No, we must decide where it falls on a *spectrum* of mild to severe. For example, does the child's (or adult's) not paying attention occur sometimes or constantly? That makes a huge difference when making a diagnosis and treatment plan. (What kid (or adult) doesn't pay attention sometimes?)

Bullying is not different. *The only way* you can correctly evaluate whether you have a parental (or other) bullying problem requires that you think of your bullying behaviors on a *spectrum*. Where do you fall on the spectrum? Do you bully sometimes, always, or depending on the week (day, minute, second) and what else is going on?

You can, of course, discover what might trigger your sometimes, always, or depends on bullying behaviors. And yes, most definitely, you can decrease those occurrences. I feel deeply grateful to anyone, parent or not, who looks hard enough, deep enough, and with enough love to want to be kind, not just when it's easy, but when it's awfully hard. Children, because they require so much, can make it hard. I hope this book makes it easier for you.

Let me know. Ask me questions.

Always best, drb

Introduction

There are days I can't even bear my teakettle screaming at me. Oh, I mean enjoy its singing to me. Just substitute the word child for teakettle and it's not so different from how you might variably respond to your child on any given day at any given moment. I don't really think the teakettle has the power to cause me to perceive it as screaming or singing. No, it's on me.

And it's you, my fellow human, who brings so many of your perceptions to your child's daily life. He doesn't really have the power to have you perceive his boiling points one way or another. No, it's on you. And, since children are open to learning all they can, they are learning you.

You are not only observing your child but he is also observing you . . . very closely. Every directive you give to him is not just a directive, it is also an unspoken message carried on the wings of your tone. The challenge for you as a parent is to learn to be in continual control of your behaviors and their concomitant tones as you provide love, and its unpopular partner, discipline. Make no mistake, discipline is love, just in a form I am hoping you will grow more comfortable with as you read on.

The challenge for you as a parent is to continually learn to be in control of your behaviors.

In order to remedy the preponderance of bullying we are collectively experiencing, it is not enough to look at social, economic, familial, and educational influences. You must look inside yourself to learn if you might be bullying yourself because if you are, you will be doing the same to your child. Most parents would rather die than think they are bullying their children.

Therefore, it is important to know you can't help your child past the point of your own conscious development. For example, your ability to forgive yourself genuinely for a misdeed, meanness, accident, ugly outburst, or other error in judgment, will enable you to forgive your child more genuinely for her misdeeds, meanness, accidents, ugly outbursts, or other errors in her judgment.

You: How can I gain control of my unconscious actions toward my child?

Dr. B. 1. Learn how you might be bullying yourself and your child. See chapter 2 of this book.
2. Use the Eight-Step Parenting Method outlined in chapter 3 of this book.

You: That's it?

Dr. B. No, learn to structure more Time Ins than time outs as they are described in Chapter Five.

You: What are you talking about? What is a Time In?

Dr. B. The very common discipline tool known as time out focuses on *remediating* your child's non-compliant behaviors (at best). What I am offering in chapter 5 is a new parenting tool I call Time In. The Time In tool focuses on *preventing* your child's non-compliant behaviors as much as possible.

You: Show me.

Dr. B. Happy to.

Dr. B. One more essential thing: Listen to your child really hard.

> Ella Fitzgerald is sixteen years old and it is Amateur Night at the Harlem Opera House:
>
>> *"The next contestant is a young lady named Ella Fitzgerald . . . Miss Fitzgerald is gonna dance for us . . . Hold it, hold it. Now what's the problem, honey? . . . Correction, folks. Miss Fitzgerald has changed her mind. She's not gonna dance, she's gonna sing."*
>>
>> —Sid Colin, *Ella: The Life and Times of Ella Fitzgerald*

You: OK.

Dr. B. Oh, one more thing. Listen to yourself really hard; it'll make listening to your child a whole lot easier.

You: From what you've written so far, it seems like paying attention to unconscious as well as conscious attitudes and behaviors will be required. I imagine this will take more parenting time and I'm usually in a hurry, so is there a short cut to this unconscious stuff?

Dr. B. No. But what will eventually be shorter is the need for as many time outs, and the time between feelings of disconnection between you and your child will become shorter. And, without question, you and your child will have happier days.

You: Seriously?

Dr. B. Seriously.

CHAPTER ONE

Parent Without Bullying

"It is better to conquer yourself than to win a thousand battles. Then the victory is yours. It cannot be taken from you, not by angels or by demons, heaven or hell."

—Gautama Buddha, *The Dhammapada*, (Chapter 8, 103–104)

I loved my mother as much as a child could love a parent, and she loved me as much as a parent could love a child . . . and then some. The then some, no question about it, was problematic, but we'll get to that later.

On various occasions my mother would say to me, "You'll be the death of me yet." I wondered, "How could she possibly know I sometimes wished for her disappearance via myriad means." Of course, that wish was reserved for those special occasions when I felt she was particularly abusive. I'm certain she would recollect those moments as instances when I was particularly challenging. No doubt both interpretations had validity. Mine, of course, more.

Did she really bully me? Yes, and often. But deep inside me, I knew she didn't want to, I knew she couldn't help it. So I picked her flowers and wrote her love cards. And in those moments when she received them, she quieted.

Deep inside me, I know you, too, don't want to hurt your child. The words in this book are my flowers and love cards to you.

Perhaps you're wondering how or why a book for parents could have the word bullying in its title. Bullying is such a harsh and unpleasant word. It makes us think of nasty, violent, and cruel things, like a bullwhip brandished by slavers or the bloody torments in bullfighting, not to mention memories of our own experiences with bullies. It makes us wince.

> We've known for years that many parents bully their children.

Yet this word is essential to understanding a new approach to parenting that I've evolved over years of clinical practice with parents and children. We've known for years that many parents bully their children. We know about child abuse and domestic violence that can result in child protective services intervention, parents being penalized or even arrested, restraining orders issued, and children taken from their homes.

What this book is about, however, isn't those extreme cases but rather a different and less obvious level of parental bullying. It is about the unconscious bullying parents inflict upon their children, without knowing what they're doing or why. Bullies—whether parents, spouses, siblings, educators, politicians, or religious leaders—don't bully because they really choose to bully. I'm not suggesting they don't need to assume responsibility for their destructive actions, because they do. But I am suggesting we need to develop a broader understanding of what motivates their choices to bully.

Another important point: The currently used and accepted definition of bullying in children is, "Aggressive behavior that is intentional and involves an imbalance of power and strength, is repeated, or has the potential to be repeated, over time."[1] This definition needs to be fine-tuned in relation to what I feel is a restricted portrayal of the concept of intentionality. So let's talk about intentionality and its impact on bullying.

Did your mother intend to seriously hurt your feelings when she ignored you for a few days? Yes and no. When you yell at an employee do you intend to demean him? Yes and no. When you ignore your spouse's request for a hug do you intend to devalue her? Yes and no. When you tell your child she is ridiculous for feeling fearful do you intend to squash her trust in her own feelings? Yes and no.

It is this *yes/no duality dance* of intentional and unintentional contradictory messages that keeps us from being clear with ourselves and each other and causes so much inadvertent collateral damage in our relationships. Bullies of all ages and designations are no different regarding their sets of dual intentions. Do they mean to hurt you? Yes and no.

---

1 stopbullying.gov

Intentionality and Behavior

There are at least two levels of intentionality when it comes to behaviors—conscious and unconscious. One of the main goals of this book is to help you understand and accept that you are a Bi-Conscious being. Our conscious behaviors are the ones we regulate. We evaluate a situation, think it over, feel about it, and decide what we want to do about it even if we decide to take no action. Our unconscious behaviors are the ones generally motivated more by impulse than thought, even when we think we thought about doing something. I'm not referring here, of course, to autonomic responses such as breathing, coughing, and heart rate.

"I don't know what made me do it; it seemed like a good idea at the time," is a commonly heard remark that exemplifies this reference to unconscious behavior. With unconscious behaviors, our intentions for those behaviors are not in our awareness. They are the ones that manifest as our lamentable behaviors. The bully is no different except he is not so quick to admit regret for his behaviors, which doesn't mean, however, that he doesn't feel any. For too long we have ignored the bully's unconscious intentions because we have, for too long, ignored our own. And what a display of communication static when both our unconscious realities meet! The inter-dependence between our unconscious realities and those of the bully keep bullying from long-term decline. Here's how that works:

Our personal bullying behaviors are born from the parts of ourselves we are uncomfortable accepting and, therefore, reject whether we mean to reject them or not. These rejected parts of self—our fear-filled feelings, our sense of inadequacies, our feelings of anger, sadness, guilt, and even joy—get shunted from our consciousness. Left unattended, our excluded feelings live on in our unconscious lives and can appear as our mean acts or commonly called bullying behaviors. It is the same for bullies. So, when our unconscious meanness meets the bully's unconscious meanness, bam.

And when two unconscious forces meet, no remedy for a problem is available unless one of the players comes to consciousness regarding his behavior. This unconscious entanglement keeps bullying from remitting long-term or short-term. So it's you and I, each of us individually, who are tasked with learning about our own unconscious intentions so we can take charge of them in order to achieve our positive intentional goals.

> *Left unattended, our excluded feelings live on in our unconscious lives and can appear as our mean acts or commonly called bullying behaviors.*

The less you need to defend your own unconscious insecurities that manifest as meanness (bullying), the less your child will have to defend against them too. I want you to understand that you are *intimately connected* to the bullying part of your child and he to yours. Our connections are not just the overt, easily seen ones we experience with each other, they are also the less obvious ones made from our unconscious lives.

We are all intimately and inextricably connected to the unconscious. If we try to ignore or reject it, that only strengthens its power over us. When we consistently ignore messages from our unconscious, we wind up plagued with regrets, becoming grumpy, ill, violent, impotent, or emotionally, socially, physically, mentally, or spiritually diminished. In other words, we become bullies and victims.

A bully may seem to be intentionally attacking someone she perceives to be weak, but the real question is *why* does she need to do that? Is she, by attacking others, rejecting painful parts of herself that she finds unacceptable? Is she trying to crush that which she feels threatens her tenuous and imagined sense of control and power? The question of her motives forces us to examine not only her overt actions, but her unconscious ones as well. A bully's overt aggressive behaviors beg for correction and must be addressed; yet overt behaviors are just a starting gate, an invitation to respond, whether those behaviors are our own or others.

My invitations to respond to bullies have come from my work over the years as a social group worker, special education teacher and administrator, psychologist in private practice, and corporate consultant. As well, my invitations to respond to bullies have arisen from myself. Thus, with such a broad spectrum of bullying challenges, I have come to experience the bully part of a child or an adult as energy contorting in pain and begging to be seen, cared about, and freed.

Gender and Bullying

A quick note about gender and bullying, since there is a lot written about the differences in the ways boys and girls bully. Data suggest boys are more prone to use physical means of bullying and girls tend to be more lethal with relational issues. And although statistics give us a view as to trends across populations, the bottom line regarding bullying and gender for me is this: bullying hurts us where gender doesn't matter unless the bullying is specifically about gender. One of the problems with statistics for large populations is that they never address the individual. So when being bullied, whether you're a girl or boy, man or woman, employer, teacher, family member, or friend who is involved, if you are bullied, it hurts you at your core not at your gender.

> *The bottom line regarding bullying and gender for me is this: bullying hurts us where gender doesn't matter unless the bullying is specifically about gender.*

I spent several years as a special ed. teacher in "rough" neighborhoods, and when I had to deal with a girl who was brandishing a weapon, trust me, it didn't matter to me if she was a girl or a boy. The issue was her intention regarding the weapon.

Boys can be sneaky and mean in relationships as well as girls and, they too, instigate "icing out" of others. Those who suffer from the icing out are not focused on the gender of those rejecting them. They're focused on their terrible feelings of being shunned.

I think it helps to view gender statistics and bullying in the same way we do statistics about cancer when a loved one gets that diagnosis. At the moment of hearing the cancer diagnosis, no one cares if the majority of sufferers are male or female. The only important factor is how to help our loved one deal with the trauma of the diagnosis.

Meeting Our Own Bully Selves

It's in our individual private lives and in our work-a-day worlds where we encounter our internal and external bullies.

For most of us, it seems easier to evaluate and label *others'* behaviors as *bullying* than our own. When *we* bully others, instead of looking deeper into ourselves for the causes of our unkind and unreceptive postures, we often tend to defend them . . . usually self-righteously!

But we must look more deeply into ourselves, since it is our own internal bullies that enable our external bullies to flourish. Again, it is *imperative* to explore beneath the surface of bullying and look, without judgment or recoil, at our personal inner lives since that is where we house our *bully and victim selves*.

I have never met anyone who doesn't have a bully/victim self tucked away in his unconscious life. I have met those who think they don't, and they are our most dangerous fellow travelers. If you were not a victim of your own unconscious internal bullying, you would not fall prey to others' bullying of you nor would you bully.

If the following self-bullying behaviors are simply one-offs, it is not a big deal, but do note them. It is when self-bullying becomes a pattern that it becomes a true concern.

Here are some examples to help you recognize self-bullying:

1. You beat yourself up for a mistake longer than any human should. For example, if, *"I should have visited*

her," becomes a mantra of self-beating rather than a simple fact, it's self-bullying.

2. You think a request is a demand and automatically fulfill the request without thinking whether it's in your best interest to do so.

3. You feel *tiny* in groups of equals and thus shy away from participating in them.

4. You feel too stupid to answer a question because you doubt you could be right.

5. You stay home from events because you feel too fat, too thin, undereducated, overeducated, your clothes aren't good enough, and you won't be liked.

6. You think you're a phony and everything you've accomplished is of no value, although you are actually quite valued by others.

7. You say yes when you mean no, and no when you mean yes, because you are fearful to assert your truth.

8. You do not ask for things you are entitled to ask for, such as a raise, a kiss, a vacation, or simply a day to yourself.

9. You incessantly volunteer for everything even when you are exhausted.

10. You don't honor proper limit setting with yourself, such as you drink too much, eat too much, spend too much, gamble too much, or pick at your cuticles so much that they bleed.

11. You don't set and keep proper limits for yourself and simultaneously feel that it is *others* who walk all over you.

12. You feel *immediately guilty* when you're asked to explain your behavior, even before you've had a chance to really think about the question.

13. You constantly fail.

14. You take or make phone calls from a person who devalues you in almost every conversation you have with her.

15. You are accident-prone and there is no physiological reason for it.

16. You find every conceivable excuse not to do the tasks you need to do to complete assignments.

17. You perpetually sound like a victim and blame everyone and everything for your plight, except yourself.

18. You scan your daily life for any dot of negativity that will support your expectation that disaster is always just around the corner.

19. You get *secretly happy* when a friend, family member, or colleague suffers. Not because you wish him harm, but because it gives you an opportunity to offer him help. You furtively know that your offer to help him is *from* your need to help, not *for* his need.

20. You still keep dating someone who is not treating you respectfully.

21. You cannot apologize for even the tiniest infraction you've committed.

22. You allow your partner to decide everything because you simply want to avoid engaging with him.

23. You *know* your friend has betrayed your trust and pretend she has not.

24. You are unwillingly silent in the face of nasty comments made to you.

25. You accuse another (partner, friend, or family member) of wanting too much from you while simultaneously giving to everyone else.

The writer Anaïs Nin so eloquently noted, "The personal life deeply lived always expands into truths beyond itself." My view of this, for our purposes here, looks like the following:

> *When you can identify your unconsciously destructive, non-compassionate behaviors and develop compassion for those pieces of yourself, you will then be able to develop more compassionate and empathetic responses toward others, including bullies and victims—be they children or adults.*

Since we are *unconsciously* engaged with life much of the time, let's learn to harness this remarkable source of power and see what really drives us so we can contribute to raising the collective consciousness of our time. We must not be afraid to ask ourselves hard questions. It requires not speeding past the truths of ourselves in pursuit of quick fixes that keep our souls untouched and unchanged.

Self-questions are not really that complicated. It's the answers that scare us because they might imply we need to make a change in our status quo. The following are examples of self-questions you might tend to shy away from because they could necessitate that you make an uncomfortable change.

After you read each of the questions listed below, think about your answers; note what you feel about them; think about what actions to consider in relation to your thoughts and feelings; and consider your thoughts and feelings as *real and important*, as opposed to letting them slip away.

Examples of Self-Questions:

- Who bullied me when I was a kid? This is hard for many of us to consciously acknowledge if the bully we remember is a parent or sibling, since our ties to family members are so deep and complicated that it makes contemplating a change with any of them terrifying.
- Why didn't I tell him he has no right to speak to me like that?
- Why did I scream and get so defensive when he disagreed with me?
- What stops me from keeping the limits I set with her?
- Do I feel free to be me in this relationship?

- I want to so badly, why can't I just quit?
- She treats me like crap, why don't I leave?
- Why don't I like my own child?
- I know he gives me a lot, so why do I keep complaining he doesn't?
- Why do I feel empty when my daughter isn't home?

We all have the options of if, when, and how we make our changes. But, make no mistake, you get to choose, and your choices will determine the texture, tone, and quality of your life and all the lives your life touches.

So let's try not to be scared of our answers or what our unconscious intentions might be. What you'll discover in staying open to self-questioning is more of you. And the more of you that you can learn to love, the more of your child you'll be able to love. The more you grab hold of your unconscious attitudes and behaviors, the more you will provide a less chaotic environment for your child to live in, which, of course, means he will be better able to learn . . . anything.

Learning you—what an incredible privilege. Socrates responded famously when he was asked to stop preaching self-examination or be killed, "The unexamined life is not worth living."

For me, the unexamined life is not quite living. It's drifting from event to event, and those events are often distractions from knowing yourself more honestly and intimately. The worst you'll find in exploring your hidden agendas are old pains and clues about how to stop bullying yourself and others.

To help you diminish your fears of self-exploration, to help you become more aware of self-bullying, and in support of what, I believe, is your intrinsic capacity for empathy, you will find that all the examples used throughout this book demonstrate how you can become more conscious of your bullying self, how to transform it, and establish more consciously compassionate interactions with yourself and your child.

With your growing knowledge of inner bullying, you will learn to

- ☐ Identify your personal barriers to your hidden thoughts and feelings.
- ☐ Check that your unconscious "static" is not intruding into your relationships.
- ☐ Manifest your true intentions as much as possible.
- ☐ Analyze bullying situations as *objectively as possible,* so you can:
    - ▶ Hear what the bully is *really* asking for.
    - ▶ Stay present (mindful) in a bullying situation.
    - ▶ Be conscious of your words, their tone, and your body language.
- ☐ Understand what authentic empathy really is and what it feels like to give and receive it.
- ☐ Constructively channel your anger with bullies.
- ☐ Enjoy the beauty and power of self-love.
- ☐ Become a *conscious* regulator of your intentions.

Loving Your Children

I know without reservation that most parents love their children very much and, on their deepest inner levels, want to "do right by them." They don't consciously intend to bully or otherwise damage them. But they do. Thus, they need to improve how they communicate their wishes and disappointments to them. Most often they're eager to learn how to do that, even if they resist at first.

As those who thirst seek water, parents become fervent about learning the differences between their unconscious and conscious intentions when they "get" that the knowledge leads them to positive outcomes with their children. It thrills them and makes parenting a bit more as they had hoped it would be.

There have been some parents, however, who don't seem to have the love I describe above.

There are parents who sell themselves as loving and well-intentioned but whose actions tell another story. That other story is the one that fascinates us and can lead to tragic headlines, like the death of Caylee Anthony, or less famous "unfortunate occurrences" that neighbors discuss in the street or after church on Sunday. Not as beastly as some horrific drama depicted in tragic headlines, but on the scale we deal with daily, those other stories of everyday bullies contribute to our general dismay with human hypocrisy.

It's still always a bit of a shock to me when a parent won't help a child, even when shown how to do it. I was working with a teenage boy, Carl, whose self-esteem was nearly completely destroyed because his mother, Amy, put him down every chance she got. In one particular tirade, his mother was complaining about, among her child's other life-long offenses, Carl's texting.

I asked Amy to make an effort to differentiate between Carl's frequent texting and Carl as a person. I made it a point with Amy, as I often do with parents in general, to make the distinction between the judgment of the child's unacceptable behaviors of the moment and the child as a valued and loved human being. I said this every chance I could with this mom since she had the habit of calling her child a loser freak whether it was about texting or anything else—the way he talked, walked, chewed his food, combed his hair—she didn't seem to like anything about what Carl did or said.

"No, I can't do that, because I disapprove of Carl as a person," Amy said. "I don't much like him and won't say otherwise."

"Your support as his mother," I explained, "is vital to Carl's ability to focus on his schoolwork and improve his grades."

"Sorry, he's an ungrateful little bastard and I'm done with him. I don't care what happens to him."

I pleaded, "Well . . . could you just for the moment, pretend to care?"

She was silent.

Amy's words and actions actually matched. She professed no help and offered none. Her intentionally cruel withholding of love and support was shocking. It's hard for us to believe a parent would *actually* choose to hurt her own child, even though she says she wants to. We see it. We hear it. And as much as we hate to admit it, it's not that uncommon. Parents often do withhold love and support as a punishment technique.

Every so often Amy, especially in public places like school meetings or family social events, declared she wanted the best for Carl and would do anything to help him. Yet Amy's attempts to sustain her image as a good parent often sounded very defensive and bore no ring of truth.

Amy refused to see herself as a bully. She refused to take any real responsibility for her unconsciously driven destructive bullying. She complained that Carl was the bully and it was completely up to him to change. Period, end of story. Did Carl hate his mom? Yes. Did he try and hurt her, yes. These two were indeed locked in a mutual bully and victim relationship, flip-flopping those roles from day to day. It was ultimately Carl who learned about unconscious intentions and was able to transform his behaviors to save himself and revamp his other relationships. Amy, unfortunately, never stopped bullying Carl. In a million ways, she remained unable to control her unconscious need to destroy Carl's self-esteem in her effort to keep him intensely and antagonistically dependent.

To be clear, Amy did "sacrifice" for Carl. She had earned graduate degrees, had a well-paying job in communications, and was able to provide Carl with travel experiences and many educational and social opportunities. She did give to him materially and did tell him, artificial and stilted as it sounded when she tried to say it, that she loved him. All her acts of giving felt cold, but they did come from somewhere deep inside her where a tad of love still flickered as a suitable yet unattainable notion. In this sense of Amy's doing "the best she could," I felt and saw her defeated, unintentional life. It was painful to see Amy try to do right in one breath and sabotage it in the next. Like a Shakespearian heroine with a tragic flaw, Amy had the tools available to remedy her bullying of Carl but she just couldn't use them.

Amy's advantages and abilities should have allowed her to understand the concept of unconscious intention and its effects on behavior. She did, actually, understand—intellectually, that is. But emotionally, she was frozen, trapped in a noticeably staccato-like, pained body, unable to reach across her fearfilled interior barriers, which blocked her from accepting her unconscious motivations for her own destructive behaviors.

Amy never accepted any treatment for herself and moved to France for business, leaving Carl ostensibly on his own from his college days forward.

The next example is of a family who sent their nine-year-old boy, Roger, to boarding school. Although, in this case, it doesn't look like parental love, it was an act of love for them to send him away, since they explicitly had no interest in finding a way to adore Roger. And Roger was adorable. It wasn't just that they wanted him out of their sight; they had concern that they would damage him further if he stayed. They would have.

His mom, Elisabeth, hated him and his father, Edgar, did whatever the mom told him to do. Elisabeth simply found her child to be in the way of her life. She was highly successful, wildly social, and rarely home. When she was home, it seemed she was surprised to find Roger there! He wasn't a welcome sight and she had no qualms about casting him, his words, his actions, and his interests out of her life. Edgar watched and took no stand on anything. Basically, although Elisabeth and Edgar were married, he functioned as a handsome escort.

In boarding school, away from his bullying parents this dear, bright, funny boy flourished. Once Roger was out of their way, his parents were able to be kinder to him. Elisabeth and Edgar provided Roger with a very comfortable material life and saw him on school holidays and vacations . . . when their schedules allowed. It was always polite and superficial, but it worked.

As noted in the introduction, one of the goals of this book is to help change the prevailing emphasis of dealing with children's emotional realities from time outs, which focus on *remediating* non-compliant behaviors, to **Time Ins**, which focus on *preventing* non-compliant behaviors.

Time In (chapter 5) is a self-esteem enhancing tool for children and adults built on the premise that the more you are able to control and manage your attitudes and behaviors, the stronger and better you will feel about yourself. The stronger and better you feel about yourself, the better you will treat others. Most importantly it is a tool to help you create a non-bullying way of life. It is a reminder that empathy and compassion for yourself and your child requires that you take the time necessary to pay attention to the nuances of emotional realities.

The Time-In Space which we'll discuss in chapter 5, can be used anywhere, at anytime, and it is not limited by physical structures. It's a protected space designed to help preempt the escalation of little, worrisome acts from becoming major bullying experiences and to reinforce positive interactive experiences. Time-In Space can be integrated into many areas of society, including schools, corporations, and religious and governmental institutions, but most importantly into your home.

Furthermore, a Time-In Space is not a room for psychotherapy, but rather a designated space where people *know* they can express the little things of any kind that are causing them distress and they will be heart-heard. If a child needs to share her joy in a protected way, Time-In space welcomes that need as well. It is a space where *empathy, compassion, and kindness are to be expected*. This isn't a program to replace counseling services. It's an ancillary system of care accessible to all who respect its rules.

Time In, as a tool and concept, is dedicated not only to raising awareness of the bi-conscious nature of our emotional, mental, spiritual, and behavioral lives, but I am hoping that just the name, Time In, will be a constant reminder for you to integrate that awareness into daily actions with your children and others—be they bullies or victims.

Self-Regulation

It can be highly destructive for us and for those close to us when we miss moments to self-regulate.

Remember the definition of bullying I referred to earlier: *aggressive behavior that is intentional and involves an imbalance of power and strength, is repeated, or has the potential to be repeated, over time?*

Think of that definition as it refers to you as a parent. I know you don't want to bully. But do you have the ability, in a challenging situation, to modulate your own actions to achieve positive outcomes?

Here's an example of parents who had to grapple with their initial pattern of inability to self-regulate. Allison is a ten-year-old girl whose eight-year-old brother, Timmy, bullies her all the time. He has been bullying her since he was two years old and she was four. He throws things at her, interrupts her most times she tries to talk to anyone or they to her, and pounces all over her no matter what she is doing.

Allison continually appeals to her mom and dad to stop Timmy from bullying her. Most often Allison's parents suggest that Allison give Timmy some leeway and "just not get into it" since he's younger and doesn't know better. And, because Allison is mild mannered and a sensitive little girl, she kept giving Timmy breaks . . . until she turned six. At six years old, Allison began to get sullen and withdrawn and the once happy, spirited child only appears when Timmy is not nearby.

Timmy is quite active and bursts into everyone's conversations, not just Allison's. Both parents think he's adorable and hardly ever step in to correct him. Allison, by age seven, tried to protect herself by yelling at Timmy and hitting him back when he hit her, for which she got punished. It's all so terribly unfair to Allison and she knows it, but she is in a no-win situation in this unconsciously permissive environment. If she ignores Timmy, as her parents continuously demand, she loses self-esteem and has no protection or validation of herself or her reasonable perceptions of reality. If she strikes back she gets punished. Timmy knows that what's happening is unfair but he is learning to love his power in the family dynamics.

Allison, now age ten, has become more sullen and, hardly speaks, and when she does it's in a whisper. She tries to sabotage her brother by either destroying something he's built or blaming him for just about every wrong thing that occurs, especially for something he didn't do. This infuriates him and delights her.

Allison has become mean-spirited, secretive, tense, and cunning, where once she was happy, open, and relaxed. Timmy, now eight, has become a bully, and his school has asked the parents to get help for him. It would have been wise of them to have stopped the two-year-old from bullying his four-year-old sister so, by the time they were four and six years old and eight and ten years old, respectively, the bully/victim relationship might have healed.

But that's not what happened. Instead they reached the point where the school asked them to bring the problem to me for help.

There were many distinct moments when choosing to be more permissive or restrictive regarding their children's behaviors were choices Allison's parents could have made with more care. They didn't see the warning signs that their children were out of balance and suffering unnecessarily since they didn't know what those signs were. They were also unaware of what was driving their unconsciously biased responses to their children.

So much pain could have been avoided.

The good news is this family was open to getting help once the school brought Timmy's bullying behaviors to their attention.

Much of Timmy's bullying was due to the fact that he was having trouble focusing in school and felt stupid compared to the other kids. He couldn't sit still and was fidgeting all the time. He had a battery of psychological tests and was found to suffer from a mild case of ADHD. Timmy received meds, individual therapy, and tutoring in math. Soon after the interventions, he became better able to control his behaviors and improved academically. And as Timmy learned to control his behaviors and succeed in other ways, the bullying of his sister decreased significantly.

Allison enjoyed individual therapy and joined a basketball team, where she began to find accolades and appreciation for her talents. As she grew more confident at sports and was well-liked by her teammates, she found her voice. And when Timmy began bullying her less, she became less aggressive toward him.

Jane and Bob, the parents in this case, each had to ask self-questions. They each had to learn why they seemed to prefer Timmy more than Allison. What was it about Allison that seemed to repel both of them? Why didn't they correct unjust and cruel patterns in their children's behaviors? At first, it was just expedient for them to have Allison indulge Timmy's abuses of her since she was older.

But in our work together, we discovered that Allison had become exactly like Jane was when Jane was growing up—angrily meek, fearful, shy, and grumpy. Jane remembered how *her* mom often hit her and was so controlling she hardly let Jane say a word without contradicting or finding fault with her. Jane's mom was routinely violent, especially when she had too much to drink. Jane realized it was safer to be silent than risk another fight with her mom, which always ended with her defeat.

For Jane, Allison became her rejecting mom. The more Jane rejected Allison because of that, the more Allison became like Jane was when she was a little girl. Jane hated seeing that and in pushing away that truth she simultaneously pushed away Allison.

When Jane became aware of her unconscious dance with Allison she was able to change it. Their new connection, devoid of Jane's history with her mother, became easier for both, and they have grown to like each other.

When you correct children, you are demonstrating your love for their physical, mental, emotional, and spiritual well-being.

Allison's dad, Bob, simply didn't want to do anything different from Jane, since he was terrified of her and had no idea what was involved with parenting. Bob came from a family where his dad left when Bob was two years old and his mother let him do whatever he pleased. Now, in his little family, any conflict sent Bob to the garage where he tended his cars.

Nevertheless, I am happy to report that Bob *did* want to learn why he had fled the normal responsibilities of being a father, especially when, and how, to discipline his children in harmony with his wife. All the members of this family are now more able to self-regulate. It was gratifying to see how the love that directs their learning became palpable.

Seizing the Opportunity

Each slap, insult, pinch, or hurtful dialogue from one sibling to another is not necessarily "kids just being kids," if these behaviors bruise egos and are *continuous* hostile patterns. If children slap each other or call each other nasty names from time to time, these are natural occurrences and can be invaluable teaching opportunities for everyone involved.

Good children's behaviors, bad children's behaviors—it's all opportunity to show that neither can topple your self-control to manage love as a warm embrace or resolute, limit-setting opportunity.

When you correct children, you are demonstrating your love for their physical, mental, emotional, and spiritual well-being. Make no mistake, children actually love to be disciplined. Here's an example of a teenager I treated who was yearning for discipline:

Sophia received no conscious parental discipline whatsoever. Unlike her classmates, she had no home curfew, no restrictions on where she could go after school, or with whom, and no one regularly checked her homework. Sophia secretly longed for limits, so she made them up. If a friend said she had to be home at 10:30 p.m., she said she did, too. Not only did she say she had that curfew but she mimicked the resentment of it as did her friends who really had the curfews.

Sophia's dad had died when she was seven years old, so she grew up with her mom, an unpredictable, emotional mixture of too hard, too soft. At some moments she was inflexible, as when she demanded Sophia go with her to the supermarket, the movies, the diner, visiting, or to the beach. She routinely iced Sophia out if she resisted wanting to go—not just not going, but for not wanting to go.[2]

---

[2] Williams, Kipling D. "The Pain of Exclusion." *Scientific American Mind*, January 1, 2011.

But there were other times when Sophia could do as she pleased. She asked to stay up late to watch shows during the week. No problem, her mom let it happen. She stayed in her room whenever her mom was home. Her mom asked her to come out and she didn't. No repercussions. When Sophia got into trouble at school, her mom never held her responsible. She always blamed the other kids, the school, the teacher, the assistant principal, the principal. The more Sophia defied school requirements and rules, the more her mom defended her. But she was beginning to resent it. Sophia was becoming a pain in the ass for her mom, and for Sophia her mom was getting to be a sad cauldron of love and hate.

With no real, consistent consequences for her behaviors, Sophia became a know-it-all to compensate for not really knowing what was expected of her. She had no reliable barometer for how to manage her attitudes or behaviors, and she became a dreaded student in her school while yearning to fit in and be like the other kids. She wasn't like them, but she tried to be by inventing lies not just about limit setting at home but about her family's having more money than it did and going to places she'd never been.

At first, Sophia talked to me as if she had no expectation of being heard. She raced through her stories as if they were decoys blocking her truths. She had been very successful with that technique with other adults. But when she realized I actually listened to her, really did want to know how she felt about things, and had no hidden agenda, she began to trust me a tad. With that initiation of trust, we began our journey of unmasking the defenses of her fragile heart, mind, and soul. I was very clear about needing to know all the factual details of her experiences as well as how she felt about each one.[3]

One of the most important components in helping this girl take responsibility for her lies and irrational behaviors was that I embraced the good, bad, and ugly parts of her with empathy, compassion, and kindness. At the same time, and with those same feelings, I provided the necessary limit setting for her.

For example, one night, as I had asked her to do, Sophia's mom finally notified me that Sophia was not yet home—it was 12:45 a.m. and Sophia's curfew was 10:30 p.m. For Sophia, now a senior in high school, ignoring her curfew was frequent. In this instance, Sophia ignored her mother's several calls and texts.

Once aware of the situation I began to call, email, and text Sophia too, to no avail. After my final inquiring text to her, at 2:00 a.m. I was no longer inquiring but asserting the parameters I had decided to set for her. I told her that if I didn't hear from her within the next twenty minutes I would notify the police since I was worried about her well-being. Within seven minutes she contacted me and after one more subsequent scenario of my texting to her to inquire as to her whereabouts, she never missed being in touch with me again when I reached out.

I worked very closely with everyone at Sophia's school, because I often do work closely with schools and because I wanted Sophia to know I was watching her. For

---

[3] Often when parents are busy, they compromise on hearing all the *details* of their child's experiences. Understandable for sure, especially from time to time, we just don't want it to become the norm as opposed to the exception.

every academic, social, and behavioral action she took and didn't, she was answerable to me. Oh yes, she bucked and was defiant, but my job was to help her change her old destructive patterns of behavior.

As I became Sophia's rock, she became more authentic. My consistency in modulating my responses allowed her to become less anxious and more honest, since she was relieved of not having to process my unconscious agenda as she had with her mom's. The reason for my ability to modulate with Sophia wasn't just because I am a psychologist, but it is also because I spend a lot of time working on transforming my own unconscious issues.

Were there moments in her treatment that I wanted to express immediate anger at Sophia for flagrantly disregarding her responsibilities and commitments? Yes, indeed. However, in those trying moments, when I reminded myself of how lost, lonely, and desperate a child she was, I found my strength to become calm and choose a response best suited for the specific moment.

It's hard to self-regulate in relation to a bully, be it your child or anyone else, especially if you still carry unconscious, unprocessed memories of having been treated unfairly by your own parents.

Let's say that you received very unfair punishments as a child and when you tried to say so, no one cared. Perhaps you dropped your glass of milk on the floor and your punishment was both to see your mom throw whatever she was holding across the room and losing your TV time. It seemed so unfair to you, after all, it was just an accident.

But you could tell by your mom's face and tone that she didn't seem to care how you felt since these were her typical responses when you had accidents:

"You did it, you pay."

"I say what's fair or not fair."

"Shut up!"

"I don't really care what you think."

After a while you stopped saying how unfair you found the punishment and just *took it,* since you had no choice.

Now you're an adult, and there's an opportunity to respond in a bullying situation where you witness a victim suffering from both verbal and physical abuse. Your gut reaction is intense anger at the bully for delivering this treatment to his victim. You will identify with the victim, as so many do, and be unable, therefore, to properly evaluate the situation. In this bullying situation, it will be extremely hard for you to transmit the compassion and empathetic responses necessary to handle the situation for both the victim and the bully, unless you have processed your history of unfair treatments to you.

The following are concepts that will help you process that history and become more comfortable with your unconscious:

- ▶ Accept the unconscious as real.
- ▶ Accept the unconscious as a significant power in your life.
- ▶ Learn what the unconscious can do *to* you.
- ▶ Learn what the unconscious can do *for* you.

- Learn why the unconscious scares you.
- Learn why the unconscious attracts you.
- Learn that the unconscious holds your personal keys to freedom from destructive habits.

How the Unconscious Helps and Hurts

We all have a bias. We're partial to the material world because we can see it and manipulate it. What we don't know, we don't seem to value as much and the unknown frightens us. Every new discovery educates us as to our limited state of knowledge, and this should keep us humble. For example, one of our most recent discoveries shows us that our universe is a lot more complex than we had thought it was.

This is from NASA: "It turns out that roughly 68% of the Universe is dark energy. Dark matter makes up about 27%. The rest—everything on Earth, everything ever observed with all of our instruments, all normal matter—adds up to less than 5% of the Universe."[4]

Awesome.

We are each a little universe unto ourselves and must humbly acknowledge how little we know about ourselves, and particularly about our unconscious selves, just as we, now, humbly acknowledge how little we know about dark energy and dark matter which seems to constitute 95 percent of our universe.

---

[4] "Dark Energy, Dark Matter." *Science.nasa.gov*. Science Beta, Dec.16, 2016.

Simply because you can't see the unconscious doesn't mean that it's not there and affecting you. It's like ultraviolet light. You can't see it, but sunbathe too long and your sunburn will let you know it's very real. Same with carbon monoxide: You can't see or even smell it, but inhale enough of it, and it will kill you. Similarly, you can't see your unconscious, but you sure can feel its effects on your life—especially if you ignore it.

Drinking too much, getting sick, and embarrassing yourself is an example of how your unawareness of your unconscious motivations makes you pay a price. After each drinking episode you feel awful and ask yourself the same question, "Why did I do that again?"

Your answer: "I don't know."

A lot of people don't care to know, but many do. And for those who do the answer is clear. There's something in your unconscious that keeps you doing what you don't want to do anymore.

Often our *intentions* are to "do good" but we wind up "doing bad."

When I was a special education teacher in a public school in a tough area of NYC, I worked with children who were part of a gang. They were younger than teenagers and known as the Baby X's.

I was trying very hard to win the trust of these little gang members so I could influence them to become a helpful gang whose members assisted the vulnerable people in the neighborhood. One day the principal of the school, who had heard another gang was coming for an afternoon territorial fight, made an announcement over the school's public address system.

"I hear the Y's (another gang) may be headed here after school," he said, "and I want you all to know this: I forbid gangs."

My class and I were speechless, and we all began to laugh. We looked at each other through the blast of unconsciousness that had just swept in from the loud speaker. In that moment, we knew the lack of consciousness of our principal. The children, of course, had no idea what to label the principal's announcement, but they knew it was, to quote one child, "ridiculous."

What the principal had revealed was just how frightened and helpless he must have felt about dealing with gangs. He wasn't a stupid man and often offered some reasonable solutions to difficult situations. In this instance, his conscious intention in the face of this potential gang violence was to protect his students and faculty. But his actions contradicted those objectives. He was of no help because of his inability to accept his fears, process them, and find meaningful solutions that might have been beneficial for school personnel and students.

Immediately after hearing the principal's announcement, concerned staff got word to him to make sure he alerted the police so they could increase their presence around our school and its surrounding area. We knew the threatening Gang Y was based in a neighboring school, so we suggested that the principal alert that school's administration of possible trouble brewing.

Subsequently, our principal made another loudspeaker announcement which indicated that the police had agreed to increase their presence, the other school had been notified, and most of the staff would help usher the children to safety after school let out. No incident materialized.

I couldn't get the principal's announcement out of my mind, so when I saw him I asked, "Don't you realize that forbidding gangs is impossible?"

"Well . . . I did think it was a bit 'off,'" he said.

"What possessed you to say that?"

"I don't know."

I admired his honesty and the power of his unconscious.

To further illustrate how lingering unconscious patterns can hurt you, here's an experience I had with a patient who was suffering with what she termed her out-of-control children. But also please note that this is an example of how the unconscious can help you!

"My seven-year-old, Tammy, is the worst child and I hate her," Jennifer said when she first came to see me, "but Bret, my four-year-old, is pretty good and so cute. I adore him."

Jennifer ached with the frustration of feeling that nothing could ever change Tammy or improve their mother-daughter relationship. Jennifer felt that everything she had tried had failed to change her disobedient, nasty child. On top of her failure to find a way to have a reasonable parenting experience, Jennifer's mom was constantly telling her that she was the worst mother she had ever seen.

I met Jennifer's mom, Lorraine, since she was willing to come in and talk about how awful she thought Jennifer was as a daughter and as a mother. I got a first-hand picture of what it must have been like for Jennifer to grow up with this mom. Resembling many parents who mean well and are unable to give authentically, Jennifer's mom was suffering from a narcissistic personality disorder.

What that, in essence, means in this instance, is that everything was about Lorraine. There was no hint of demonstrative empathy, for anyone unless she thought it would get her an accolade or a boost to her imagined status. She flew into rages if she felt slighted, and her asking for anything was actually a camouflaged demand that she get whatever it was she was asking for. Her callousness, when she felt injured from an imaginary or real slight, was awful to hear. Lorraine didn't limit her negative judgments to her immediate family. Everyone in her line of vision was grist for her judgmental evaluations.

At first, Jennifer didn't cry about how hard it was to try to please her mother. She hated everything about her mother and wasn't shy about expressing her anger at her mother's selfishness. She didn't really want to spend too much time talking about her feelings about her mother. She spent our early sessions screaming about how much she hated Tammy. But in time, I found the right moments to reach her interior places of emptiness and terror, which had originated with her mom's utter unavailability as a nurturer.

When I expressed empathy about Jennifer's growing up with Lorraine, she began to cry with the pain of feeling that she had no mother. She confessed that she had stopped caring if she had a mom or not and simply had become accustomed to using her own abilities to survive and, eventually, become a successful lawyer.

As the floodgates of her collected reservoirs of pain opened, out walked a softer, more loving Jennifer. And as her frozen heart thawed, she felt guilty about her inability to love Tammy. It was at this point she really "got" how inappropriate she had been as a parent—no consistent limit setting, no real hugs, twisting her children's arms, smacking them, and constantly screaming at them. She "got" how she had become a missing mom.

Jennifer realized she hadn't ever really embraced Tammy's fragile, vulnerable self, since she had abandoned her own so many years before. The innocent child, Tammy became the recipient of Jennifer's rage at Lorraine's narcissistic limitations of motherhood.

When Jennifer became aware that she was responding to Tammy as if Tammy were her own mother, she was able to change her parenting behaviors. Tammy, according to Jennifer, "became a different kid." Of course, it was Jennifer who had become different in order to institute changes. She began to set limits for Tammy in a real way and implemented consequences when Tammy defied her or broke a rule. This took a long time to institute, since setting expectations and implementing consequences regarding attitudes and behaviors had been virtually non-existent in this home.

After the changes were made and results clear, Jennifer became crazy about Tammy. She now experienced Tammy as someone with whom she loved to spend time.

As Tammy was becoming a fabulous kid, however, Bret suddenly became the terrible child, the one Jen started to now hate and the one for whom Jennifer saw no hope of changing. Jen, started to use the same sentences to describe Bret as she had used to describe Tammy's "horrible, immovable behaviors and wretched, mean personality."

I reminded Jen of that fact, and explained how her unconscious blockages were still so strong that she couldn't see (until I pointed it out) that her frustrations and feelings of helplessness and hopelessness regarding Tammy were *exactly* the same ones she was now experiencing in her parenting with Bret.

And you might be wondering, "Where was the dad in this family?"

For a long time Jen didn't want to talk about her husband since she was so beset with her unmanageable children. She brushed away my inquiries about him as not relevant since she felt he was such a dud dad and beyond help. I pointed out that if she felt that way it made all her parenting tasks more difficult and we should get into it. We did.

It seems as if Greg, Jen's husband, adored Bret and actually wasn't such a dud when it came to spending time with him. Greg was a playwright who worked from home much of the time and Bret was his little companion. Greg played with him happily and showered him with affection and treats, the very things he didn't share with Jennifer. Jennifer was so busy with her law practice and "the kids" she hardly paid attention to how she felt about what was missing for her from Greg or what the children were missing from him. Until now.

As Jennifer transformed her anger into conscious gestures of love toward Tammy, her perceptions of Bret as a threatening horror child remained and had three lingering sources. One, she still held vestiges of anger at being a pawn in her mother's narcissistic drama, which she now projected onto Bret. Two, she felt hurt and angry at Greg for withholding his love from her and shirking his responsibilities as co-disciplinarian with their children. And three, she was jealous of the love Greg showered on Bret.

Once Jennifer realized she was jealous of the affection Greg showed to Bret, she was able to acknowledge that she wanted Greg's love, too. In the past she had treated Greg as she did her mother, by pretending he wasn't there and he didn't matter. He did. She missed the Greg he was when they first married; she realized she missed the Jennifer she was back then, too. It was becoming clear to Jen that Bret was just a little boy who was the recipient of way too much affection from his dad's unconsciousness and way too much anger from his mom's.

Jennifer began, again, to mourn for the hurt, lonely, lost girl she had been, and for how the feelings of rejection and abandonment she lived with from those past pains helped generate the chaos and bullying of Tammy, Bret, and Greg.

Greg knew Jennifer had a short fuse, yet he loved her and his family no matter how volatile and violent their home had become. When he understood that it was Jen's unconsciousness causing her to be so explosive and that she was getting help with it from me, he agreed to work on the marriage and parenting issues with Jen. Greg also began to work on his own unconscious issues. This delighted Jennifer and she, spurred by Greg's renewed commitments to her and the children, re-committed herself to the marriage in a more authentic way. That reinforced Greg's love for her, so this family became functionally, emotionally, and spiritually happy. Predictably, in time, Tammy and Bret's self-control issues improved both at home and at school.

In this case, we can see the powerful, tenacious grip our personal histories can have on our perceptions and experiences, including how we perceive and respond to our children and, consequently, shape their lives. Through the lives of Jennifer, Greg, Tammy, and Bret, one can feel the reality of the power in these words of Carl Jung, *"Until you make the unconscious conscious, it will direct your life and you will call it fate."*

Did this mom have unprocessed rage regarding not being heard by her own mom? Yes. Did she fly into a rage when her children didn't listen? Yes. Was her husband unconsciously weak and frozen? Yes. Was it fixable? Yes. But, it takes homework on your interior landscapes for the fix to work.

At this juncture, I hope you're beginning to realize that the unconscious, to which you are inextricably and divinely tethered, is a source of unremitting guidance. It's your prototypical parent. It will pester you until you learn what you need to know to help you have more balance in your life regarding any particular situation.

Think of it as you would a repetitive dream that keeps waking you up until you understand the message of the dream and take positive actions in relation to those messages (the repetition stops when you take the right actions). That's how powerful, supportive and awesome your unconscious is in finding ways to try to help you.

I'm always delighted when children bring their first dream to therapy, since it's usually so useful in revealing what's wrong. Dreams of adults are too, but I'll start with this child's dream since it's hard to miss its message and easy to see how a child's unconscious can help bring information and enlightenment for the purpose of change.

In her first dream twelve-year-old Isabella was sinking in quicksand. I've found that children frequently dream of being buried alive when their identities are being crushed. Fortunately, Isabella's family brought her for help even though they hadn't yet grasped just how much she was suffering.

I asked Isabella to create her dream using self-hardening clay. When she was finished, it showed only a dot of her head above the quicksand line. Her little ego was slipping away and that might eventually portend death, or death of her identity. Either way, I had to help her develop a much stronger feeling of self-worth.

> ...the unconscious, to which you are inextricably and divinely tethered, is a source of unremitting guidance. It's your prototypical parent.

The good news is that she was not suicidal. She was slipping away in other ways and these were the reasons:

- ▶ She was different from other girls her age and found them insensitive and boring.
- ▶ Her father was totally self-absorbed, having affairs and being rarely home.
- ▶ Her mother was strong and protective, but angry and short-tempered due to the fact she had four children, a job outside the home, and was the only responsible adult in the house.
- ▶ Her mother and her siblings suspected their dad was having affairs, which he did not deny.

This is how Isabella got better:

- ✓ When I asked Isabella if she could now make a picture of someone reaching down to help her out of the quicksand, she could. Prognosis—good.
- ✓ She learned to value her wonderful level of sensitivity and not take the insensitivity of other girls personally. She stopped withdrawing when kids bullied each other and found courage to speak up against bullying.
- ✓ She accepted that she preferred to play sports after school and not go shopping for outfits she didn't care about.
- ✓ She enrolled in an art class on Saturdays and loved it. She found other kids there who shared her sensitivities.
- ✓ We built a rocket together and when it was done we shot it off in the park near my office. The focus the whole time, obviously, was of energy going powerfully in the opposite direction of quicksand.
- ✓ Her mom and dad came for counseling and developed ways to support and cherish Isabella's artistic, athletic, and unique personality.
- ✓ Her mom and dad agreed to live together but accepted that they were not suited as mates. This allowed them *both* to be more present at home and take the time to learn each child in a more authentic way so that their unconscious hostilities were no longer flying around the house.

✓ Isabella has grown to become a wonderfully accomplished artist and is adored by both her parents and siblings. She now has a young family of her own and is a fantastic mom. So simple was this little girl's dream, yet it told so much.

A dream has so much to give to you. It's a special delivery letter just for you. How can you possibly resist opening it?!

When patients and I interpret dreams together I'm continuously impressed how the most pertinent information regarding their lives has traveled from the depths of their souls' night journeys into their awakening minds. We discuss the dream at length, with the patient free associating to the images in the dream to discern its message. I assist with my knowledge.

How do we know when the meaning is correct? We all know, doctors and patients alike, when we feel that click inside that says, "Yes, this is right."

A dream has so much to give to you.

Sometimes interpreting the dream is like buying shoes. When the first pair isn't quite right you keep trying on other sizes and styles until you have exactly the right pair. It's that click of "yes" about a pair of shoes, a person, a school, or a therapist that we feel when we know it's right. And it's the same with interpreting your dreams. You "know" when you're on the right track.

Here's another example of the profound enlightenment that came by way of a child's dream while I was teaching her in school.

Eight-year-old Dena was a shy, quiet, sad, seemingly distant young girl, who always let others have their way. She was a good girl, way too good of a girl and, therefore, a candidate for serious victimhood down the road. Encased in an amorphous cloud, not seen but felt, she went about meeting class requirements.

I couldn't seem to make a real connection to her. I was having trouble touching her heart.

I did, however, "connect" with her through academics, but she still felt far away. And although she's the kind of child teachers love because she causes no trouble and does everything they ask her to do, I couldn't bear being unable to make my connection with her more real. I didn't want her to go through her school life untouched and unchanged except for her fine academic progress and being labeled *such a good girl.*

I was so distressed, that one night I prayed very hard for a dream to help me touch Dena's soul and inspire it to come alive.

That very night Dena appeared in my dream, wearing a white dress with a veil on her head that flowed down her face and back. She looked sullen and zombie-like in her movements.

I assumed, because of her age, that this white dress was a religious first communion outfit. Why did my dream show me this religious vision of her? What responsibility was this child expected to newly take on? In *real life* Dena does appear so pure and weighted down. My pain, and now this dream, told me I had to do more for this child.

I pursued my concerns with Dena's parents about how programmed I thought Dena seemed, and how extremely obedient she was. They were delighted she followed classroom and school rules and was being such a good girl. I carefully suggested that she didn't have to be *so* good all the time and they thought that a bizarre statement coming from a teacher.

What I discovered in discussion with Dena's parents was that her family was extremely religious and much of their family life centered on church and church-related activities. These folks were also becoming more prominent in their church and their need for Dena to be a perfectly behaved, good girl became abundantly clear. For Dena's family, being good seemed not just about being good but about how goodness keeps away the wrath of God.

I had to do a better job of focusing my attention on finding different ways to ignite Dena's soul, make her laugh, show her that mistakes are normal, and help her experience the joy of spontaneity. I had to transmit to her that everyday life was not just a set of rules to follow but a wonderful journey full of surprises. I wanted her to say no to someone, say no to me, and initiate something that sprang from her own being, other than needing to use the rest room.

For every occasion my class could possibly celebrate, I used grab bags as an activity to help reinforce the fun of surprises. We had a mistake story day. On mistake story day, the children had to create a story in which someone (or some animal) made a mistake, and then we discussed ways to fix it if it could be fixed or accept it if could not be fixed.

"Oops," became our most fun word and completely overused by all, including me. I made sure to make mistakes and model dealing with them in a fun way, no matter the outcome of the mistakes. Mistakes are friends, not enemies.

At moments I thought I saw the flicker of more life in Dena's eyes. But I still wasn't convinced I had touched her soul in a way that truly made a difference.

Then, at the end of the school year, Dena brought me a picture of herself in which she was wearing a white confirmation dress, veil and all! On the back of the photo she had written, "To Miss Becker who is even in my dreams." I was speechless and, in that brief moment when our eyes met as she handed me the photo, I saw her eyes alive for the first time. It was pure joy. She knew I knew, and in that place of purity where words diminish meaning, none are needed. I had touched her soul and my prayer was that, with that touch, others might have the opportunity to do so as well.

The same nurturing relationship with your unconscious life via your dreams awaits your attention. Enter into this relationship with the excitement and openness of a child at play joyously discovering . . . everything.

Your unconscious knows you will stumble, fall, ignore its wise advice, have tantrums, and be mean. But it won't give up on you or let you slide from its relentless care, just as you won't give up on or let your child be denied your undying love.

Parenting provides ample opportunity to grow with your children. And for those with grown children, ample opportunities still remain.

CHAPTER TWO

Bully Parenting in Action

A Native American elder once described his own inner struggles in this manner: "Inside of me there are two dogs. One of the dogs is mean and evil. The other dog is good. The mean dog fights the good dog all the time." When asked which dog wins, he reflected for a moment and replied, "The one I feed the most."

—GEORGE BERNARD SHAW (1856–1950)

Parents are vital accomplices in either perpetrating bullying or remediating it.

Parental bullying that is blatantly apparent and easily identifiable, such as physical abuse, sexual abuse, or obvious neglect, is *not* the main focus of this chapter. Although these are surely sorrowful examples of parental bullying and have grave consequences, they get a lot of media and breaking-news attention.

The focus of this chapter is on the everyday parental bullying behaviors, which undermine children's self-esteem, tear at the internal fabric of their souls, and create the number of bullies and victims surrounding us.

The Flexibility of the Brain

In case you feel overwhelmed by the thought that you can't change old stubborn parental bullying habits, here's some up-to-date information about the flexibility of the brain from Sharon Begley, noted author of, *Train Your Mind, Change Your Brain:*

> *Research in the past few years has shown how the adult brain retains impressive powers of "neuroplasticity"—the ability to change its structure and function in response to experience. These aren't minor tweaks either.*[1]

So, although you may stumble at first when searching for more compassionate responses to your child, you can be reassured that your old negative brain patterns can most definitely be changed as your new more empathic responses displace them. I know that even in the most intense moments of disciplining your child, it's your authentic empathy for her that will make or break your effectiveness as a parent.

In Sy Montgomery's wonderful book, *The Soul of an Octopus: A Surprising Exploration into the Wonder of Consciousness*, she quotes her octopus expert friend, Scott:

---

1 Begley, Sharon, "The Brain: How the Brain Rewires Itself." content.time.com, July 19, 2007. [Back Cover].

> *Just about every animal, Scott says—not just mammals and birds—can learn, recognize individuals, and respond with empathy. Once you find the right way to work with an animal, be it an octopus or an anaconda, together, you can accomplish what even St. Francis might have considered a miracle.*[2]

To parent without bullying, the requirements are the same—to learn, recognize your child as a unique individual, and respond to him with empathy. Accepting the naturalness of your child's rage, love, fears, guilt, sloppiness, distractions, pains, sorrows, joys, unbridled energy, unrelenting begging, forgetfulness, etc., is to acknowledge that it is up to you to find the right way to work with him. He will respond.

To find the right way to work with your child implies there is a wrong way. There is. But correcting the wrong ways is your ticket to joy in the miracle of a moment. Therefore, you must look at the wrong ways without judgment or shame but with gratefulness for the opportunity to grow and become more than you were a minute ago.

The Powerlessness of Children

Children, by definition, are naturally needy and dependent. They are, therefore, easy prey for parents to consciously or unconsciously bully.

---

[2] Montgomery, Sy. *The Soul of the Octopus: A Surprising Exploration into the Wonder of Consciousness*. Atria Books, April 5, 2016.

Children have no real power in relation to you, the parent, especially when they're young. This is why it's vital for you to modulate your emotional realities with kindness, compassion, and knowledge of the differences between too little, too much, or just right parenting in daily life. You can think of this as the Goldilocks Approach to Parenting if we have to give a name to Bi-Conscious decision-making for parenting.

For example, your nine-year-old daughter is having a screaming, crying meltdown. Her body is shaking with rage. She's filling the air with ear-splitting screams with intermittent accusations that you're always unfair and she hates you.

What do you do?

1. Tell her to stop screaming or be sent to her room for a time out. Too hard.

2. Explain that you mean well and she shouldn't say she hates anyone, especially you, and you love her so much. Too soft.

3. Walk away until she stops screaming and acting up. In this instance, too hard. In a different situation, this might be a "just right" action.

4. Just hold her. Too soft.

5. Tell her if she stops crying and screaming she can have the play date with Susie. Too soft.

6. Since she's out of control and it feels real to you, not manipulative, do hold her (soft) and let her know she is safe and you do want to hear what's triggered

this level of pain and distress (strong). Here you're being both soft and strong (hard).

7. When your daughter begins to quiet, find out what exactly you did that made her feel you were unfair. If you agree and can see why she believes you were unfair, authentically apologize. If you don't think you were being unfair, and she did something that was against a rule, after the discussion about it, invite her to come up with behaviors that might have brought a different outcome for her.—Just Right.

8. If your daughter experienced you as being unfair and you don't think you were, it is also possible that you had unconscious anger attached to your directive, thus triggering your daughter's anger, which then led to the escalated situation.

The above item, #8, is quite a common occurrence and one of the main reasons limit setting fails. When parents' feelings of anger or frustration are attached to a directive they give to their child, it clouds the directive *and thus* the child doesn't feel corrected, she feels bullied. If neither parent in a particular situation understands the power of the effects of his own unconsciousness on his actions, their child is left feeling emotionally defeated and confused. If it's one parent in a particular situation who doesn't understand that his unconscious tone may be attached to his directives, it is to that parent the child will feel estranged due to his confusion about the mismatch between his parent's words and tonality.

It is easy to see that your child's daily experiences of confusion and emotional defeats, created by accident of your unconscious tones, can be perceived as, and experienced by your child as, bullying.

Here's another example that illustrates how little power a child actually has. Let's say a child receives continual bullying in the form of dismissive insults from a parent. For example:

> "Just leave me alone and get out of my room."
>
> "I don't care what you think."
>
> "If I say pick it up, pick it up! I don't have time to tell you to pick up the damn shoe again. Next time you leave it in the hall, I'll throw it out and you can explain to your teacher why you only have one shoe."

What are the child's options? Usually, if a parent is consistently bullying he is not generally open to his child's objections regarding his parenting attitudes and behaviors. As well, there's nothing actionable for anyone to call the police about, no observable external marks to cause anyone concern, and not necessarily any obvious immediate changes in the child's academic or social behavior to warrant school intervention. Since most children are too afraid to run away, they suffer in lonely silence as the impact from the constancy of their parent's bullying mounts in them over time.

It's important to remember that just a few moments of your child feeling disconnected from you due to a harsh, unconscious insult from you, can feel like forever to him. A dot of despair in any heart matters, and it especially matters in a little person's heart.

Children are trapped, forced to sustain bullying insults and other forms of abuse, unless they somehow remove themselves from a bullying parent's presence. Parents are often surprised when their usually compliant child begins to act out his frustrations and get into various troubling episodes when he becomes a preteen or teen. Sometimes a child's acting out in negative ways starts much earlier, it depends on the nature and intensity of the parental bullying.

If your child doesn't run away from you physically in his attempt at self-protection, he may run away internally by indulging in various maladaptive behaviors. Symptoms common at preteen and teen times are anorexia, bulimia, obesity, cutting, alcohol and drug consumption, electronic device addiction, cyber-bullying, cyber-stalking, stealing, failing grades, and staying for long periods of time with other families instead of at home.

Parents run away from discord, too. I'm always amazed with how many parents give their children "the power" to render them helpless, ineffectual, or out of control. You don't need to be a professional to notice when a child is running the show!

No child really wants his parent's uninvited "power." That unwanted "power" is his parent's *unassertive power* that he absorbs by default of his parent's ineffectual parenting. It will enhance your perspective and real strength as a parent if you remain aware that it's not your child who has the power in the parent-child dyad—not in size, physical strength, knowledge or social skills . . . at least not when he is young. It's you!

Owning Your Power

To parent without bullying is about owning your parental power with as much conscious authority, empathy, and compassion as you can on any given day in as many moments as you can. I know it's not easy, since we all can effortlessly slip into unconsciously unkind behaviors when we are upset. So I'm going to offer some real examples of parental bullying from my work with parents and children to help you identify what those behaviors might look like. If you recognize any as your own, you'll know you need to transform those bullying behaviors. And if these examples don't fit you exactly, think for a moment about some of yours that might.

The following are said in nasty, threatening, and demeaning tones. When you think of your own bullying moments with your child, remember it is often your tone that creates the sense of fear and trepidation in your child.

Here is a list of some parental bullying statements:

1. "You selfish little spoiled brat."
2. "Get in here right now or there will be hell to pay."
3. "See this belt? I know how to use it. You'll listen."
4. "That's it, I'm calling the orphanage and you're out of here."

5. "I really don't give a damn what you want, this is what we're doing, so shut up."

6. "Never ever tell anyone what goes on in this house. If I find out you did, I'll rip out your tongue."

7. "Don't even dream of opening your mouth again, I said NO, and I mean, NO."

8. "You're really such a loser."

9. "You look like a fat pig, that's why no one wants to date you."

10. "I don't give a shit what you do. You want to drink, drink. You want to stay out all night, I don't care. I've washed my hands of you."

11. "You're a little bitch. Apologize right now!"

12. "It's not my fault these games are always on days we're busy. Be grateful you have a nanny. Not everyone is so lucky. Don't be so selfish."

13. "So, he hit you, get over it. Fight back next time, don't be a sissy."

14. "Of course, you're not included, nobody likes you. It's your own damn fault you didn't get invited. You think you're so special and you're not."

15. "Why did you get a B? You told me you studied? Did you lie about that?"

16. "Why won't you go to school on parent's night, again this year?" the child says. "It'll be a good report."
"I know. That's why I don't feel the need to go."

17. "Sit here! You may not leave this table until your homework is done. If you have to go to the bathroom, I'll go with you because I don't trust you for a minute. All you'll do is text Larry. Larry won't help you get into college. You won't get into anything but a crap school if you keep up your damn texting."

18. "Phony as she might be, I simply don't believe the assistant principal would say that to you. So stop lying about her."

19. "Yeah, I'm glad you won the game, but it's not that important in the scheme of your high school work. Win or lose, it's all the same really. Just focus on your schoolwork."

20. "Is it so much to ask you to do what I ask today, can't you see I'm doing the wash? After all I sacrifice for you, I would think you wouldn't even dream of not doing what I ask of you."
    [Note—This child tends to this mom everyday in a multitude of ways including: polishing her nails, combing her hair, going shopping with her, doing the dusting, washing or drying the dishes, and escorting her to social functions.]

21. "If you don't put the iPhone down right this minute, I will shut off the service. I'm not asking you again."
    [Note—The parent threatens this every day but never shuts the service.]

22. "What the hell do you see in that loser? Is that the best you can do?"

23. "Tell me, damn it! I hate how you withhold everything. No? Fine. Don't ask me for anything. This has to be a two-way street or you can get your own meals and wash your own clothes and I won't tell you a G-d damn thing either!"

24. "I told you to get out of my office while I'm on the phone. I only ask once, so now you'll pay. I'm leaving right now so I don't smack your face, you can fend for yourself, big shot. One day, if you keep this disobedience up, I might leave and never come back. How'd you like that, Danny boy!"

25. "Oh my darling, I'm so sorry I said that to you and in that icky way. Please forgive me. I wasn't thinking and I just had a horrible conversation with Aunt Betty and I was so 'off' from that. I'm truly sorry."

The last comment (#25 above) would be a fabulous way to start to repair the severed connection you, no doubt, initiated if you went bully-bonkers with your child. It happens! If it isn't your pattern to go bully-bonkers, but a periodic exception to your relating, it's generally no problem. In fact, it can be a most helpful teaching tool if every so often you make an insulting remark or blow your child off with a dismissive gesture.

This is how it can benefit you and your child when you sometimes bully-parent.

▶ You are perceived as human, and can apologize in a real way, which implies you are 100 percent present with your eyes locked into the presence of your child.

- ▸ Your heart-felt apology can bridge the disconnection you helped to create with your insensitive comment or gesture, and you get to compliment your child for her graciousness in forgiving you (when she's ready), which enhances her self-esteem.
- ▸ You model the fact that no one is perfect and that does wonders for your child's self-expectations. To err—so human; to forgive, so human.
- ▸ So *just fix your bullying error* instead of

  1. Pretending it didn't happen.
  2. Accusing your child of imagining it.
  3. Getting angry at your child if she didn't like *your* angry-bullying behavior.
  4. Claiming your child is just too sensitive for her own good.

Bullying Yourself—Bullying Your Child

As you read this section keep in mind forgiveness. The child, inside of you or outside, deserves empathy, compassion, and applause for learning.

"But I'm insecure about parenting and that's why I f--k it up so often."

That's something I often hear parents say when they feel that they are failing at parenting. The reality behind that common sentiment is twofold.

First, it's true that many parents are, indeed, insecure about parenting, since many didn't have great role models and the teaching tools offered to them are often globally prescriptive and don't require them to examine the most important parentally destructive aspect of themselves—their unconscious agendas.

Second, many parents who claim to be insecure about parenting are actually just insecure overall and parenting is just one more place they demonstrate it. It's often the lack of a positive rapport with the unconscious that renders us insecure about much of life. Without self-knowledge and consistent examination of motives, fears, shame, and low or fluctuating self-esteem, we become uncertain about many of our choices, be they for our children or anyone else. And when we're ambiguous about our decisions, we often state them without conviction (too soft) or with aggression (too hard) instead of simply assertively (just right).[3]

The ways you might be bullying your child are the ways you, no doubt, have been bullying yourself, unless you have worked to change your bullying behaviors. For example, your parents became cold, hard, and inaccessible when they didn't like something you said or did. Now you become cold and hard when you don't like something your child says or does.

Self-bullying, as noted at length in chapter 1, is so important to recognize, because it *motivates parents to bully unbeknownst to themselves.*

The following few examples from chapter 1 reveal the *specific connections between parental self-bullying and the bullying of a child:*

---

[3] Please note the Goldilocks approach to parenting can be utilized in many other domains.

1. You beat yourself up for a mistake longer than any human should. Connection: You beat up on your child for a mistake he has made and you don't stop harping on it.

2. You don't ask for things for which you are entitled. Connection: You don't foster assertion in your child and when he does assert you criticize him as unworthy to have asked for things he has asked for.

3. You are highly self-critical for being too fat, too thin, not smart enough, and unsure about any decisions. Connection: You are critical of your child's weight, intelligence, clothes, activities, etc.

4. You say yes when you mean no, or no when you mean yes when you are fearful to assert your truth. Connection:

    a. You hesitate giving a clear directive to your child.

    b. When your child makes a clear choice, you question it and question it and question it.

One by one we bully. Two by two we bully. Three by three we bully. A thousand by a thousand, a million by a million we bully and thus the Archetype of the Bully is born. Our collective experience of demeaning others grows to a force that kills individuals one by one or thousands by thousands . . . millions by . . . , because we comply with self-righteous defenses of our own bullying behaviors.

We don't do this by active consent. We do it by default to our unintentional, unconscious behaviors. How ordinary it's become for us to cast "the other" into a label of devil or demon if he doesn't do what we want him to do or threatens, in any way, our fragile feelings of security.

We are all but human sufferers, afflicted with our own unconscious agendas.

This "other," whom we instinctively designate a demon, can be a person who has acquired that status simply because he doesn't look like us, has a different moral compass from ours, is from a politically different group, is culturally a mystery to us, or is our annoying acting-out child. It is important to remember that we often label that which frightens us and makes us feel helpless—a demon.

We are all but human sufferers, afflicted with our own unconscious agendas, and that knowledge should help us see others as multi-faceted beings, not just as simplistic unidimensional witches, brats, bastards, killers, horrible people, or incorrigible children. I am reminded, here, of a wonderful line from the preface to the play *The Time of Your Life*, by William Saroyan: *"Despise evil and ungodliness, but not men of ungodliness or evil. These understand."*

It's hard to be compassionate about others' unconscious lack of kindness unless we are able to compassionately understand our own.

We may not have experienced the pain of an addict who's trying to kick a compulsive habit of decades. We may never experience the hungers of a criminal who steals. We may not have experienced the life of deprivation or abandonment a bullying parent has endured. But what we *do* know is that there are reasons for desperate acts, and judging the needy, the afflicted, or the tormented is unkind. All of our houses are made of glass.

Most importantly, it is in the sustained intimacy of your embraces with your child, be the embrace a hug or one of limit setting, that you teach your child what it feels and looks like for one person to understand and respect another. That truth, simple as it sounds, will have a huge impact on your child's respect for himself and, therefore, others.

It is through *you*, whether you bully or do not, that your child will become enabled or not to help diffuse his own potential violence. In this regard, it is easy to see the power you posses as a parent not only to diffuse your child's bullying as it will, no doubt, occur in daily life, but to see how your acts of dismantling his bullying make a significant contribution to decreasing violence in your extended family, with neighbors, and, thus, to our society. *You are the key.*

The Bully, as an archetype, will lose its potency for each of us as we each transform our individual bullying attitudes and behaviors. Eric Garner's life mattered, Michael Brown's life mattered, Officer Wenjian Liu's life mattered, as did Rafael Ramos's life matter. An Israeli child's life is precious and a Palestinian child's life is precious. Your life is precious and your child's life is precious. Let's take a look, now, at how you translate the love you feel for your child into conscious, respectful, daily expressions of permissions and restrictions so that each of us, ultimately, becomes less likely to be perceived as a projected symbol of someone else's unowned rage.

CHAPTER THREE

An Eight-Step Parenting Method

Tell me and I forget. Teach me and I remember. Involve me and I learn.

—BENJAMIN FRANKLIN (1706–1790)

Here are steps to take to help you parent without bullying:

Step One—Identify the Problem

Start with just one specific behavior that's causing conflict between you and your child. Don't try to deal with everything at once, just pick the worst thing going on and save the rest for later. Once you've figured out a way to reduce or eliminate one big problem, the rest will become easier to approach as well.

For example, your daughter is being resistant, avoidant, and won't listen to direction. She is also oppositional, pouty, belligerent, angry, and sloppy with her homework. Simultaneously, you can't bear her non-compliant behaviors. You get irritable, impatient, condescending, judgmental, and insulting toward her. Basically, you bully her as you try to get her to comply. Problem identified.

I'll use this Dreaded Homework Situation as illustrative of the Eight-Step Parent Method in a bit, but here are the rest of the steps so when you read the homework example you'll be able to identify the steps as you read.

Step Two—Acknowledge That You Sometimes Bully

Even the best parents do. Parents are people too, human! What I am aiming for is to decrease parental bullying behavior incident by incident.

When your child is out of control and you'd like to either smack him or say mean things—stop yourself. That's a great start. Use your anger level as a clue that this is the moment you could go out of control. Think—"I'm getting loud . . . I can feel my heart pounding . . . my breathing is too fast . . . " and let that be your signal to check why you may be going emotionally out of control. Ask yourself these questions:

"What am I feeling, other than hating what my son is doing?"

"Am I tired?"

"Do I have a cold?"

"Did my husband just insult me?"

"Did I lose an important account at work?

Answer:

"Yes I'm tired, frustrated, and hungry. This is when I 'lose it' and become that mean-spirited bully-parent I hate to be. Oh my God, I can't believe what I've been doing. I'm the worst!"

No, you're not "the worst" anything, just a parent trying not to bully so much. Recognizing you do is fabulous. That's a major step on the way to parenting without bullying.

Step Three—Identify Your Own Internal Vulnerability Triggers

Why am I so angry? Who is this child to me now? Am I acting as if she's my angry sister, horrible sixth grade teacher or mean grandma? Does she remind me of my mom who never heard me, my big brother who stole my toys, my dad who slapped me if I didn't do things fast enough for him? Any childhood trauma, especially if unexplored, can be a trigger source for bullying your child.

I worked with a mother, Erica, who always, and I do mean always, criticized her son for not being a good athlete. Whenever he tried playing baseball, soccer, basketball, or tennis, she was brutal toward this boy.

"Get in there and run, for Christ's sake, just f---ing run," she'd yell from the sidelines. What the hell is the matter with you?!"

Her son, Fred, invariably burst into tears and did run—right out of whatever game he was attempting to play.

When I explored with Erica why she got so irate at Fred for disliking and not being especially good at sports, we discovered that both her parents never truly supported her about anything. But there was one thing that Erica had excelled at and that was soccer. Through all her school days Erica was a star player in several sports, especially soccer, and she wanted Fred to have the same shot of developing good self-esteem from playing a sport, just as she had had. Erica was terrified that Fred would fall to pieces if he didn't have a chance of succeeding at a sport.

"After all, he is a f---ing boy!" she told me. "And I'm a girl and I would have fallen to pieces if I hadn't excelled in sports."

Whether Fred developed self-esteem through sports or not isn't the key point here. He eventually did do well at soccer, but the key point is that help for Fred came through Erica's discovering her own vulnerable trigger points that touched off her bullying her son.

The first thing Erica did after mourning her own painful childhood experiences and her guilt about how awful she'd been with Fred, was to learn how to embrace his fears about playing sports and help him through them. After she did, Fred was able to accept his mom's more appropriate coaching.

Step Four—Ask, "How Do I Control the Bully in Me?"

When you sense you are about to bully your child, stop, take a breath, think, and review what you've learned.

Ask yourself: "What has my child done to trigger this level of *anger in me*?"

For example, an eight-year-old little girl, Michelle, doesn't listen to her mom, Lisa, when Lisa asks her to do anything. Michelle not only seems to be ignoring her mom, she does it with defiance and a bit of a sadistic attitude. If she does do what her mom asks, she does it begrudgingly. It's not uncommon for your child to not listen from time to time, even with an air of defiance, but this girl's set of defiant behaviors was the rule not the exception.

Lisa had grown to resent Michelle. She had no patience with her and dismissed her complaints and objections as unworthy of addressing, other than with a punishment. The more Lisa dissed her the more Michelle defied her mom.

Finally, Lisa realized she'd better figure out a different approach since somewhere deep inside she knew she loved Michelle, and sometimes, when she didn't feel that, she knew she should. The more she felt stuck about how to deal with her daughter, the worse she felt about herself. So it went round and round until she asked the important questions, "What has my child done to trigger this level of *anger in me*? Why does she get me so angry and riled up when she ignores me?"

"How do I not react to Michelle impulsively?"

Lisa discussed this situation with a trusted friend who had observed her and Michelle in various settings. After much discussion, she arrived at the insight that released her from her negative, unconscious bond with her daughter, "Oh my God, this is about my mom who never heard me! I couldn't get through to her; she ignored me and was often a bit sadistic when giving punishments. My mom could be so mean when I didn't do what she wanted me to. She iced me out for long periods of time. Never cared if I was crying, begging for her to talk to me and listen to my side of something. Now I can see that this isn't about Michelle, who has no real power over me. Nor should I give her my power by becoming angry so easily. Now that I see she's not my mom, my anger has quieted and I'm sure I can find a way to connect with her."

When Lisa released herself from the baggage of the leftover behavioral traps from her emotionally painful childhood, she could, and did, listen to her daughter, Michelle.

To control the bully in you, especially when you feel you're about to explode, remember to talk to yourself, and listen. Helpful hints:

1. Ask, "Is this how I want to behave?"
2. Ask, "How do I want my child to perceive me?"
3. Ask, "Why am I letting Joaquin get to me?"
4. "I hate not feeling in control. What's next?"

    a. Take a deep breath, then another. Make sure you feel you're in your body. How? Feel the floor under you. Touch an object and feel it. Feel your breath find its natural rhythm. Smile.

    b. Now that you have taken charge of yourself—take charge of the moment with your child.

    c. Evaluate what your *child needs* in this particular moment. Give it. Be Clear, calm, and compassionate when you connect with your child.

5. Key phrases to remember for manifesting your self-control: Center myself, be Calm, Compassion rules and Calibrate my intentions.

6. Be proud.

Step Five—Make Sure There is a Bridge Open Between You and Your Child

This is your full-time job as a parent. It is essential for there to be a line of communication open between you and your child in order to solve any problem. Remember, this bridge between you and your child breaks all the time. It's a natural and normal part of building trust, which is why it is essential that you know how vital it is to repair the emotional ruptures that commonly occur.

This sequence of love, hate, and bridge rebuilding is natural and necessary for restoring feelings of safety and security for your child.

The frequent experiences of love, hate, and making amends in relationships can be a long-lived torture zone for some of us. So many people—men, women, and children—find themselves trying desperately to repair tears in the fabric of their love relationships. Many of us wait with an aching heart for a call from a loved one that hasn't come yet, hoping it will be the salve for the pain of the rupture in our connection with that loved one. You're not alone in this type of suffering.

The foundation of these types of pain has its origin in the wobbly parental (and sibling) bridges experienced in our childhoods. Know also, however, that as we develop positive internal bridges between our unconscious and conscious selves, the pains from, *real or imagined*, disconnections in love relationships will significantly decrease.

The psychologist, Melanie Klein, in her seminal book, *Love, Hate and Reparation*, outlines the sequence of love, hate, and the need to repair parental disconnections as beginning in infancy. She points out that an infant feels love at feeding time, then hate (aggression) when feeding (milk) is not available, and the loving bond between parent and infant is felt again when feeding returns.

This sequence of love, hate, and bridge rebuilding is natural and necessary for restoring feelings of safety and security for your child. It's normal for ruptures to occur, especially with children, and it is also important to remember that you are the primary, instrumental emotional bridge builder for your child.

Your awareness of your reactions to these normal ruptures affects how you set limits or otherwise show love. For example, if a disconnection exists between you and your son, and it feels so unbearable to you that you give him everything he wants as a way to reduce your discomfort, it is neither in his best interest nor yours.

You both may feel relief in the moment, but no authentic bridge is built between the two of you. The only lesson gained here is that your son knows how to manipulate you and you, semi-secretly, know you "gave in" . . . and it semi-secretly feels wrong. But, you felt relief in the moment and the demands of daily life proceeded as usual.

I caution, however, as time moves on your son will "up the ante" about what he wants or what he wants to do. The price will become too high for you to give him an easy "yes." Subsequently, both of you will feel helplessly estranged from each other. In time, you will discover that the unspoken, semi-secret bond which was built from your indulging your son, was established to answer your needs, not his. Both of you will carry the unspoken burden of your regrettable collusion. What to do?

Instead of perpetuating an unconsciously indulgent bond between you and your son, evaluate what *he* needs in order for him to feel that the bridge between the two of you is trustworthy and safe. If you respond to him out of your needs, as described above, the communication bridge between the two of you will be rickety. But if you examine yourself and separate your needs from his, you will build a sturdy relationship bridge dedicated not to quell your anxiety, but to provide your son with a conscious, strong, and trustworthy parent guide.

Humor can be a great bridge builder since it shows that you're comfortable with what's going on and not overwhelmed with a rupture in an emotional bond. If you use humor sarcastically, however, you signal your own discomfort in the situation. So use humor with conscious thought about the needs of your child in each instance.

Here's an example of the wise use of humor for keeping a fluid communication bridge open.

A nine-year-old boy asks his dad if he can have the famous "One more time" at a game.

"Let me think if we have enough time for it," his dad says. "OK . . . yes, you can."

"Can I do it one more time?" the boy asks again.

"Now wait a minute," the dad says, "you just had one more time so, if you do it one more time, that would be two more times since one more and one more is really two more times."

The boy begins a shy smile.

"No, really. Sorry we only have time for the one more time. I love how you asked though, not whiney. Good for you!"

Here's an example of unwise use of humor:

A nine-year-old girl has been nervous about going to her grandmother's for a week without her parents. She's in a toy store with her parents and her mother sees her looking at Halloween costumes. Her mom points out the one of a witch and says, "Maybe you should get that one to take to Grandma's so you can scare away any monsters that may be hiding there."

Step Six—Remember, There is No Enemy; It's Just Your Precious Child

When you have a fight with your child, your child only *feels* like an enemy to you if you put her in that category. Without your participation as part of a "fight," there is no fight. What is real, even in the context of being angry with your child and perhaps wanting to get her out of sight, is that you are simply one precious parent wanting to guide your precious child as best you can and "fighting" is the last thing you really want to do. Your child, of course, is looking to you for guidance on how to process her uncomfortable feelings, since the last thing she wants, really, is to "fight" you. You, as parent, are the designated human transformer responsible for purifying the internal indices of your child's rages.

Here's an example. Your child is having a hissy fit because she can't go to her friend's house for a play date. You thought you had this settled two days ago when she agreed it didn't make sense to go, given everything she had to do that day. This is a moment you could "lose it," start yelling and treating your daughter as an enemy combatant. Or, you can be the transformer of her anger and disappointment. Here's how:

Always acknowledge your child's feelings first, before you attempt to teach her anything. When you feel like wringing her neck stop and remind yourself, "No, probably wringing the girl's neck is not the best parenting approach. That would be about me and what I feel I need in the moment! [Big smile!] I must think about what she needs."

She needs you to accept whatever it is she feels in that moment—anger, disappointment, frustration, anything. Sometimes there are add-on feelings when kids are frustrated, and you hear about every time you ever disappointed them. Your job is to stay calm and receptive and address your child's feelings with empathy and clarity as you lead her to the truths of your agreements regarding the play date. The sequence is clear: you receive your child's anger, transform it inside yourself, and give her back empathy about her disappointment as well as a reminder of her other commitments for that day.

That sequence of transforming your child's anger and giving back something loving is a powerful mechanism. By using it your child learns

1. Her feelings won't kill you.
2. You are stronger than her weakest moments.
3. Her feelings are not bad; she's allowed to have them.
4. She is safe in your presence no matter how angry she becomes.
5. You're a wonderful parent.

The same transformative sequence helps you

1. Keep your focus on your child's needs.
2. Have confidence that validating your child's feelings first is the key to establishing a pathway to correcting her behaviors.
3. See your child as the vulnerable precious being she is and not an enemy combatant.
4. Grow more confident in your ability to modulate your own emotions.
5. Feel strong in a real way.
6. Feel like a wonderful parent.

Key questions to ask yourself about parenting in a challenging moment to help you remember to keep your focus on the vulnerability of your precious child:

> "What does she need right now to feel better? Is it a gentle hug or a strong one?"

"Does she need me to be flexible about listening to the pains in her request, or can she wait?"

"Does she need me to repeat my directive or does it seem that she's got it."

"What are the situational variables of this moment?" For me, "Am I overwhelmed with fears because I just lost some money?" If so, you might tend to be snappier and more critical of your child. For her, "Is she hungry, tired, or did she just have a fight with a friend?" If any of these are true she will probably be on a short fuse.

The strength of your love must permeate your tones and gestures in all directives, the easy ones and the most difficult ones. If you remain calm and clear it will increase the probability your child will too, and she will, subsequently, be more likely to accept whatever decisions you make for her.

Step Seven—Know Your Child's Uniqueness

Each child, just like each octopus, bird, or flower, is unique. A successful parenting approach with one child won't necessarily work with another.

No two children are the same even if they're the same age, same sex, in the same classroom, or hate the same other kids. If there are siblings in your home, each child has a different environment to which she is reacting, simply because the other sibling is there. Home environments are often quite different from what you think they are for *each* child.

Parents don't respond to their children the same way, even if they think they do. They inevitably resonate with one child more easily than with another, which tends to make them like one child more than the other. And because parents generally feel guilty about preferring one child to another, their authenticity with each child may suffer. For example, a parent who prefers child X may give more to child Y to overcompensate for preferring child X. Or, a different parent may be totally unconscious of preferring one child more than another and simply give more to her preferred child. Subliminal as it may be, kids know your truths. Be guided by that and know that each child has a unique beauty, which, when consciously celebrated, leads to acceptance between all family members.

The unique beauty of your child is what makes him precious to you. All his behaviors—his strengths and weaknesses, his sensitivities and vulnerabilities, impulsive responses, joys, sorrows, humor—everything he does is his soul talking to yours. That is why it is so important to listen.

Take your child's emotional temperature in each moment you are able to, since the moment won't come again. Life is a series of moments and each is your opportunity to teach and be taught by your child. Ask yourself why you think your child is being non-compliant. Does she get nervous when her dad comes home? Is she afraid to go to bed? Does she like to show off or does she tend to hold back her skills and talents? How cute is she when she tosses her hair out of her eyes? Does she falter in math, reading, both, or not at all? Are her moments of meanness sweetly predictable to you just because, "It's so her?" Is she empathetic? Does she guess why you're sad?

I ask parents who are having trouble with a child to describe the child. Some are great at reporting the details of their child's assets, liabilities, quirks, and special powers of love. As they tell me about the child's attributes, they begin to radiate with that warm, special . . . parent-love-glow. Then there are parents who only tell me the details of how difficult the child's behaviors are for them. Invariably, the parents who share many details with warmth in their telling know their child well. The ones who report only the difficulties with their child focus on their reactions to the child and don't appear to know their kids very well.

Each child's emotional temperature has a different baseline, so it's important to notice the fluctuations. If your child isn't usually volatile then one day she is, your reaction should be one of concern. On the other hand, if she's generally volatile and then one day she's a bit more volatile than usual, your reaction should be, of course, of concern but a little less so.

When you are truly getting to know the intricacies of your precious child and are watching her slowly unfold to you, know that you are immersed in the miracle of creation and effecting the substances inherent in that phenomenon.

To parent . . . what a gift.

Step Eight—Check In for Feedback

After you've identified your own triggers, controlled the bully in you, communicated empathy for your child, and worked hard to reduce or eliminate a dysfunctional interaction—*stop*. Step back. See how your child is doing in the moment. Is your effort making her smile, tear up, close her eyes and hide? Does she seem more relaxed and happy, or uncomfortable, nervous, jumpy? Is she speaking softly, shouting or snapping back? Is this particular effort working with her or should you take a longer break and come back to it another time in a different setting?

If your child is upping her anger at you and escalating the nasty things she's calling you, you've missed the essence of what went wrong. Go back to the beginning of the event in question and review it carefully. You'll find the kernel of your child's escalating anger is often that you haven't admitted that you've made a mistake. If that is the case, apologize. Kids are very forgiving. Forgive yourself, too. Here, it's important to also remember that a significant common kernel of discontent within your child may not be about the directive you gave to him but the tone with which you gave it.

The purest source of feedback, obviously, is your child. Look at him, feel his tone. You'll know if you met his needs by the way he is content or not, sulky or not, and if he's relatively calm. If he's adjusting to a correction he's had to make in his behavior and he's a little sulky for a few minutes, no big deal, leave him be. If he stays sulky for hours, you may need to check in with him and find another way to reduce his discomfort.

Parents, when frustrated, are tempted to bully their child when, after having seemingly succeeded with quelling their child's meltdown, the meltdown reappears in a flash as if it had never been tended to! With the quick reappearance of a meltdown, it is common for a parent to feel *not good enough*. Parents feel awful not just because they tried so hard and failed to achieve a lasting outcome, but because *not feeling good enough is a common reaction to failure*. Thus, when parents feel not good enough it is easy to see how they can easily slip into unconscious bullying behaviors if they aren't aware of the power of their vulnerable feelings.

The following example is the composite Dreaded Homework Situation I referred to earlier. It's a *very common* situational parenting problem and it reflects the Eight-Step Parenting Method, designed to help you reduce bullying in your home.

The Dreaded Homework Situation

Dr. B.: Why do you dread doing homework with Debbie?

Debbie's Mom: Oh, it's a nightmare. She won't sit down at the table when it's time for us to do her homework, and when she finally does do it, it's sloppy. It's awful. She's a smart girl, she just doesn't focus. She becomes like a slinky toy in her chair flopping all over the place and fixing her skirt again and again.

Dr. B.: How do you deal with these behaviors?

Mom: Well, I tell her to sit still. I get angry with her and tell her she's acting like a big baby and if she doesn't sit there and do her homework with the right attitude I won't be able to read her her story later since she is robbing that time by acting so irresponsibly. Then she has a melt down and starts her crying tantrum behavior. I just can't deal with this.

Dr. B.: Of course you can. So let's take a closer look at both of you. Do you resent the requirement that you need to do homework with your daughter?

Mom: No. Not really. I just resent her being so impossible about it.

Dr. B.: I was thinking it must be hard for you to come home from work, not have a second to yourself since you have to prepare dinner, not get a chance to unwind, and then have to sit and do homework with a nine-year-old. And I know it can't help matters that your husband has almost no patience with your daughter and his job takes him to Spain for three weeks at a time. And when he calls, all he does is complain about business. He says, if I recall correctly, "Homework is your domain, I have quite enough on my plate."

Mom: [Note—Tears start to trickle down the mom's face.] It's true, I dread doing homework with my daughter. It's the last thing I want to do after a very demanding day at the office. All I can think about is finishing up with her, drinking a glass of wine, and having some time to myself! I haven't been allowing myself to admit this, but my husband just isn't comforting as a partner or as a father. And he's way too hard on Debbie. He never even acknowledges that her problems matter or that our child is hurting. *I feel so alone in my marriage.*

Dr. B.: Do you think you bring some of this frustration and sadness along with you when you approach the homework table?

Mom: Not consciously, but I do see that I'm bringing resentment of having to do this on top of . . . everything else. Wow, I feel terrible thinking I'm helping to create this daily horror and I'm hurting Debbie!

Dr. B.: I feel that, but I also know how much you love and adore Debbie and how so much of the time you're a great mom with her. So, how about having some compassion for yourself and your overwhelming reality? Fixing this homework horror pattern will just take learning what happens to your patience when you feel overwhelmed and alone with the weight of those feelings. The degree to which you feel overwhelmed with the homework situation is also connected to how desperately alone you feel in your marriage. I remember too, how terribly alone you felt as a little girl after your brother died. So, it's not just the homework that's causing you to lose your patience and insult your daughter. It's also the weight of your non-supportive marriage, your workload, and history of feeling like a lost and lonely little girl that has you tense, racing internally, and feeling frustrated.

Mom: How can I fix this?

Dr. B.: Now that you're aware of your part in this problem, we need to focus on your daughter and what she's bringing to the homework table. How has she been doing regarding other work assignments from school?

Mom: Mostly OK. But she could do better. She's very smart, everyone says so, not just me. The teacher told me just the other day, though, that she did a terrible job on her little story about her trip to her cousin's birthday party in Paris. She wrote one sentence about the candles on the cake and the chocolate icing on it, and that was it.

Dr. B.: How did you deal with that?

Mom: The teacher suggested I review the whole trip with her and maybe that would help her write a better story. She also said maybe there was something on the trip that was difficult for Debbie and she might want to share that. So, we did the review of the trip itself and Deb drew pictures of our cousin's house. She also said that her dad spent half the time at the party telling her not to eat the cake and ice cream or have a soda. So she felt like a jerk at the party because she was the only kid who couldn't have any fun food. After I empathized with Debbie about feeling like a jerk at the party, I told her I'd speak with her dad about having a little bit of the fun food at parties in the future. After the time we spent together, Deb crafted a lovely little story.

Dr. B.: Great connecting! How wonderful of you to be so creative with Debbie and help her with that assignment. You can do the same thing with her other homework. Instead of pushing her to just do it quicker and better, and becoming angry and condescending when she's having trouble, you can be there for her in the same real way you were for the writing assignment about her trip to Paris. Great work! You found out what was going on *with her*, then you joined in with her on the task and remembered that if you fought with her it would leave her feeling alone, inadequate, and stupid. You fought your own negativity and won. So here, you both felt good! Brava.

> *. . . discipline is just another form of love—when you do it right.*

I'm wondering, even though Debbie is really smart, she seems to lack confidence in doing her academic work. Why do you imagine that might be?

Mom: She's afraid of making a mistake.

Dr. B.: Why?

Mom: When her dad is home he's so hard on her for every little thing. And so is her grandma.

Dr. B.: For example?

Mom: [Note—She is noticeably upset and angry as she quotes her husband.] "Get the hair off your sweater, don't leave your hand on the table, quiet when I'm working. Get that dog out of here, I hate it shedding in my office. I will not have that piggy friend of yours in this house. Fix your blouse, girls don't walk like that, pick up the piece of paper as soon as you drop it . . ."

Dr. B.: I see, Debbie is terrified of being wrong and harshly judged. She's scared of her dad's condescending attitude and judgments, so she freezes up and can't perform. Do you sometimes judge your daughter harshly as well?

Mom: Not like her dad, but yes, sometimes I do when she won't listen and do what I want her to do.

Dr. B.: You mean like at homework time! So the key, *after you examine what you're bringing to the event*, is to look for what she might be feeling and address that, not see the situation as simply her being oppositional, since we already know that's what she's being. That's just our starting point. The fix for the homework dread is your ability to see what negativity you might be bringing to the situation, take responsibility for that, and think about what Debbie needs in order to feel better about the task at hand. If the remedy requires you to spend more time with her, you'll need to make it happen without resentment. You did a great job with the story assignment. You didn't take it personally, and, stepped right in to help Debbie deal with her lack of confidence and feelings of humiliation that she suffered on the trip and that subsequently hindered her from writing an acceptable story.

Debbie's mother came back to me a few visits later with good news.

Mom: Debbie was fabulous about her homework last night. She went off to her room and tried the assignment herself, and then she was more open to letting me check it over and help her fix a few mistakes.

Dr. B.: Why do you think she went into her room to do it alone instead of, as she usually does, at the kitchen table with you nearby?

Mom: She's an independent girl. She often plays alone in her room and creates stories with her dolls.

Dr. B.: Do you think it was self-protective because she has some lingering fear you might jump on her if she gets sloppy with her work?

Mom: Hmm, maybe. But she did a good job on her own. Maybe she just wanted to prove she could.

Dr. B.: Maybe. It's great she did a good job and did it more comfortably, and I'm certain that your being more relaxed about homework helped her enormously.

Mom: Hmm, thanks.

The key tool, whether you're happily hugging or seriously disciplining your child, is you. It's your responsibility to set consistent positive and corrective consequences for your child's behaviors regarding meeting your expectations.

. . . when there's rigid commitment to one ideology, there's only a slim chance that the parent is open to his unconscious agenda.

And always remember that discipline is just another form of love—when you do it right.

It's how you deliver your comments, questions, kisses, instructions, hugs, winks, shoulder touches, rewards, consequences, strolls, smiles, tears, and laughter to your child that will make the difference between fostering a bully/victim child or not.

Yes, your child will, no doubt, be bullied or victimized from time to time. But your child will not become a victim or a bully if you check the appropriateness of your own thoughts, feelings, and behaviors as you parent daily.

Parenting Styles

Parenting styles can vary depending upon your family background, religion, ethnicity, and culture. We've heard about Asian Tiger Moms who expect their children to behave and perform according to very strict standards and attain only high grades in school. We hear about African-American parents who use more physical discipline in order to help prevent their kids, particularly boys, from behaving in ways that would provoke much worse violence, even murder, in an American culture still plagued with racism and unequal justice.

Remember also the laissez-faire, permissive style of parenting, when "be your kid's best friend" was the vogue among marijuana-smoking young parents of the sixties and seventies.

And of course, we're all familiar with the notorious "helicopter" parents who hover over every minute of their childrens' lives, programming them to start building their résumés at age three, get into an Ivy League schools, become highly-paid lawyers or doctors or work for big banks, big tech, big Pharma companies and so on, whether the children want to or not.

With some parents, parenting styles do exist in pure form, but in my experience many parents modulate those styles to some degree. When parents parent at the extremes of a parenting style, I find a great deal of damage. When there's rigid commitment to one ideology, there's only a slim chance that the parent is open to his unconscious agenda. It's also hard for the parent who uses a parenting "style" to parent, to change, since he finds security in the parenting "style" that he lacks within himself.

There is no one parenting style that makes sense except in a particular moment. So if your parenting style is to be as bi-conscious as you can possibly be in any given moment, I'm happy with that! Depending upon the variables in each situation, with a bi-conscious approach, you'll always be evaluating for just the right approach—not too soft, not too hard, but just right. It is definitely the Goldilocks Approach to Parenting that wins the day!

With a bi-conscious approach to parenting in mind, here's an example of how to be flexible based upon the variables in a given situation.

Let's say your child is basically great at following rules. For most of his successful rule-following you reward him warmly with smiles and hugs, and you verbally let him know you are proud of him, especially when he's first learning the rules. Then, one day, he breaks a rule he usually adheres to. What's your best approach?

Since this disobedience is an exception to his usual behavior, you can check yourself to see if you're different that day; steamed about something, not feeling well, racing past things, including him. If not, just ask what's going on with him that day. Do it warmly and let him know how proud you are of his usual great behavior regarding this rule.

Then, be extremely flexible regarding a consequence. You may decide he only needs to acknowledge his error and share what was going on for him that created this exception to his behavior.

"I know you know the rule and won't do this again," you can tell him.

A hug would be great to seal the deal. Your tone of acceptance and understanding of this unique non-compliant behavior demonstrates your ability to be flexible and that you trust him to get back on track.

Now, let's say you have a child who continues to break a rule over and over. Ask yourself if you have been clear about your expectations. If yes, ask yourself if you have been consistent regarding giving consequences for the non-compliant behavior. If no, get consistent and make sure each infraction is dealt with in a consistent manner.

Don't be defensive. Your child hasn't followed the rule, so discipline is what love looks like in this situation. Don't be flexible about the consequence in this instance because your child's proper behavior hasn't been established as a pattern. Since he's repeatedly flaunting his disrespect for your rule, this is definitely not the time to negotiate terms.

"You've broken this rule over and over so you'll be grounded for a week."

A more serious, cool tone would be appropriate here. Not a tone filled with anger or disgust, but one filled with your confidence and love for his *need to learn*.

That need is your impetus for creating further opportunities to teach him how good it feels to meet expectations. Simultaneously, it's time to find out why he's so angry and fighting you. That will take further exploration, including self-exploration. Think about it deeply. See him. What's the nature of your bond with him in general? What might be missing with your connection with him? What is he afraid of?

Regarding the above examples, it is easy to see that it is not a parenting "style" that would provide an effective reaction to your child's behavior, but it is, very definitely, your ability to consciously evaluate your child in a given moment, that will be your most valuable asset for gauging and tailoring your responses best suited for him. By learning to trust your ability to evaluate both yourself and your child in the moment you'll be delighted to find how much easier it becomes for you to set limits, modulate your emotional responses, and become appropriately flexible.

Your new level of consciousness about how *your specific attitudes and behaviors* profoundly affect your relationship with your child is *key* to building a strong foundation of authentic love and respect with him.

Parental Non-Bullying Basic Rules

Here are some basic non-bullying precepts:

- No smacking, beating, pinching, twisting arms.
- No spitting in your child's face or at any other part of him.
- No threats of abandonment.
- No threats of consequences you can't (or don't) follow through with.
- Do judge the child's behavior, not the child.
- Do set limits for routine matters for daily functioning.
- Show affection when you feel it or when you perceive your child needs some.
- Compliment your child when she deserves it.
- Always *assume* your child wants to do what is right to meet your expectations. Even when she is displaying the opposite of what you want, I promise you, deep inside of her, she wants to please you. Your job is to help her find a way back to that desire when she isn't manifesting it, because, beneath her defensive angers and other acting out behaviors, your child *would love to be able* to please you and have happy days. *Build that bridge.*
- Be *open* to the fact your child is your teacher—especially in the tough moments.

Yes, you will make mistakes, doubt your decisions, and resent your child's outbursts, especially when you're exhausted. And if you're like a lot of parents, you may tend to forget that most mistakes can be valuable teaching experiences and are quite fixable. Another very important factor to remember is that children, even in hard and toxic situations, are forgiving. They seem to have built-in empathy for their parents' pain and somehow sense their struggle to love them well. That often feels amazingly generous of them.

> ... children, even in hard and toxic situations, are forgiving.

What will help calm you as a parent and help you make your best parenting decisions is not a technique per se, or the style of the moment, or looking up what someone said about parenting. How, for example, could someone else tell you how much time your child should spend with his grandparents since no one knows them as well as you do. No, what does profoundly matter in parenting is your confidence in your non-bullying decisions. What will help your confidence in parental decision-making is your continued success with regulating your responses to your child's specific needs, which fluctuate daily, or in some cases hourly or minute to minute.

Sometimes when parents are frustrated and don't feel like disciplining their child, they say, *"Kids will be kids."*

Of course they will. We just don't want that cliché to become your hands-off parenting style! Children will always confront you, have tantrums, resent you, compel you to set limits for them, force you to punish them until they understand the limits, and receive the rewards they earn from jobs well done. Your most intense feelings of frustration, helplessness, joy, sorrow, anger, pride, fear, doubt, anguish, and guilt often come to you by way of your children. That's the gift they bring to you. If you allow yourself to be open to learning from them, they will be your profound teachers.

Opportunities also exist for you to reinforce and express your bi-conscious, non-bullying parental style by joining your child in the all-so-pervasive new opportunities of cyberspace.

Since cyberspace technology is such an integral part of your child's home, school, and extended social life, it's imperative that you take an active part in this twenty-first century reality and develop relative comfort with both positive and negative aspects of cyberspace and cyber technologies.

CHAPTER FOUR

Cyberbullying Help

*I shot an arrow into the air,
It fell to earth, I knew not where;*

— *The Arrow and The Song*, Henry Wadsworth Longfellow (1807–1882)

Texting, email, computers, cell phones, tablets, Facebook, YouTube, Instagram, Twitter, Snapchat, etc., can be dangerous and damaging bullying influences on your child. And yes, the possibility exists that your child is being cyberbullied or he may be cyberbullying others. But cyberspace fear is not new. It's only the most recent place where we experience our deepest fears of the unknown.

The internet is a fabulous arena filled with music, games, movies, social media, and educational apps. It provides so many ways for your child to enhance his eye-hand coordination, intellectual curiosity, and communication skills. It also offers yet another way for your child to experience a modicum of autonomy that can enhance his self-esteem. And you can connect with your child in all these ways.

Cyberspace offers just one more opportunity for you to say to your child, through your actions:

> "I want to know what tickles you, what makes you wonder, what frightens you. I want to connect with you, teach, comfort, and embrace you. I want to know you. I will take care of you within and around your cyber experiences as well as I do with all other experiences."

Overcoming Your Resistance to Cyberspace and the Internet

Some parents reject the positive aspects of cyberspace because it's sometimes used for highly destructive behaviors. Correlations have been shown to exist between bullying and various devastating consequences of it, such as increased anxiety, depression, school absence, and suicide. Cyberbullying is not exempt from these same manifestations of bullying consequences.

I want to caution you, however, not to throw out the baby with the bath water and miss opportunities to connect with and enjoy your child with cyber-related activities. Of course, your first concern is how to protect your child from harm in this realm, and I will review those steps shortly. But to make sure that you can remain balanced in your views and not fearful of the world in which your child participates, let's first review your relationship with

Preventing Cyberbullying

cyberspace per se. Your capacity to respond to cyberbullying experiences that may arise through your child's online activity is affected not just by the nature of a destructive occurrence, but by your comfort levels with the reality and technology of cyberspace.

Let's start with some questions about your comfort level with cyber activities:

1. Are you familiar with cyberspace in general?
2. Do you engage in the joys of the internet with your child?
3. Do you know what apps your child loves?
4. Do you research other apps for your child in the same area of her interests?
5. Do you surprise your child with new information from your searches for her?
6. If your child is playing a game on the computer, do you show interest in having her teach you that game?
7. Do you communicate with your child through, text, Facebook, email, Skype, or other online social media?
8. Do you ever say, in front of your child, "I just got an upsetting email and I'm thinking about how I want to respond?"
9. Do you share your joy at discovering new information online?

10. Do you watch movies together on a laptop or tablet when travelling?

11. Do you watch movies on a laptop or tablet when you think it would be a good moment to be close to your child and hang out?

12. Do you know that teenagers need some privacy and need to keep certain secrets from you, and that this truth can be expressed through online usage?

13. Do you ask your child to do research for you on the internet?

14. Do you praise your child's expertise using the internet to do his homework?

15. Do you know when your child's need for cyber privacy has dipped into a problem level so that you can help?

It's crucial to use cyberspace as a positive way to connect with your child so that engaging with him about and through this domain is natural—especially if there is a cyberbullying problem. When you and your child are engaged in a positive alliance regarding cyber realities it will be easier for you to monitor his cyber activities on an on-going, non-threatening basis.

Cyberspace is another arena in which you have the opportunity to flex your bi-conscious muscles and take charge to help your child feel safe regarding what her internet experiences might be. Just as with other types of bullying, how bi-conscious you are matters a lot when dealing with cyberbullying issues.

- Are your responses compassionate and well thought out? If your answer is yes, great!
- Do you seize the opportunity to comfort and delve into the details of the particular incident? If yes, great!
- Do you brush away your child's small cyber-hurts as if they are of no importance and ridicule his sensitivities? If yes, not good. Check your unconscious motives.
- If your daughter is having a troubling online experience, do you slam down the cover of her laptop and take the moment of her distress to reprimand her for careless use of social media? If yes, not good. Check your unconscious agenda.
- Do you imply that your son's addiction to social media caused him to be bullied and he would, therefore, never have been bullied if he had just closed his Facebook account? If yes, not good. Check your unconscious intentions.
- Do you take the time to take whatever steps are necessary to quell your child's fears and soothe her hurts until she feels safe? If yes, great!

Cyberbullying can feel more devastating to a child, or to any of us, than other types of bullying, due to the fact it can occur *anytime, anywhere,* and *anonomously.*

As well, cyberbullying can feel unstoppable since the bullying acts can be ongoing and spread like wildfire through your child's extended social environments.

For many parents, cyberbullying breeds more fear than "regular" bullying since it adds the element of the unknown to parents' already existent feelings of being overwhelmed. And when parents feel overwhelmed, as many do, they tend to lose their cool more easily and slip into bullying behaviors. Therefore, cyber realities do demand more vigilance and self-regulation for parents.

Noted with compassion for all of us, not just for parents: our brains can only process a certain amount of information at a time and internet availability has created a world where we get bombarded with all kinds of information all the time. How many of us have said, "I'm not watching the news for a day; it's just too much?" Many of us participate in online gossiping, blogging, and shopping. Now add to this the fact that your child is bringing home his—sometimes good, sometimes bad, and sometimes ugly—cyber experiences. So, yes indeed, the reality of cyberspace does require a new layer of watchfulness for you.

However, let me help with a perspective regarding the unknown as it relates to unexplored "space." When frightened of the unknown, we have always projected our fears onto new products in the area of communication, when those products offered *new ways of utilizing space.* Some communication products of the past that induced our fears: books, the telegraph, the telephone, radio, TV, cable, and satellites. None of these feels threatening today because we've grown familiar with them for what they are, just tools. Any tool, not unlike a pencil, can be used to create something wonderful or be used to kill.

That's it. The internet is a tool we get to use for good or ill. Each of us, in the context of our homes and larger societies, must consciously set our ethical and moral standards for internet use. As a parent, you have the power to guide your child in all space, including cyberspace.

Monitoring Your Child's Internet Activity

There is no question that your job as parent is to keep track of your child's use of cyberspace by setting rules for the use of it. Here are key things to do (some incorporated here are found on the very helpful site, stopbullying.gov).

1. Check the sites your child visits.
2. Put in parental controls, which can filter and block access to inappropriate websites using your router or third-party software.
3. Have a non-threatening conversation about sites your child visits.
4. Have a list of his passwords and advise him not to share his passwords with friends since he (therefore you) may not know the friend's cyber-safety protocol.
5. Advise him about what is appropriate and not appropriate to post. Advise him never to give his personal information, such as real name, school he attends, age, address, phone number, or calendar events on sites.
6. Engage with him about the dangers he might encounter and encourage him to monitor, as you have, what is and is not a proper site to visit.

7. You'll find that kids often know if a site should be off limits. But also know that at certain ages, kids will check out those sites anyway. As when kids used to find a copy of *Playboy* and share it with pals, these days they can, and often do, find hard-core pornography and secretly share it with friends.

8. Yes, girls do it, too.

Furthermore, it is important to share a few words about cyberstalking, as differentiated from cyberbullying, since the need for parental controls regarding cyberstalking is imperative.

Although anonymity is a key factor in the spread of cyberbullying, with its devastating emotional, mental, and social consequences, cyberstalking adds another dimension of potentially dangerous outcomes, such as physical and sexual assault, kidnapping, and even murder. Cyberstalkers easily hack computers, smart phones, and tablets to steal credit card information and other ID for nefarious purposes. They can be pedophiles who target children and racists and homophobes who use the web to spread hate and target their victims for physical attacks.

In 1990 cyberstalking became a criminal offense, and there has been a lot of attention paid to the topic in the media, such as in television's *Law & Order-SVU* (Sexual Victims Unit) and *The Stalker*, in the movie *Misery*, and in the book *Stalking Mary*, by Eileen Bridgeman Breinat. Given the ease of cyberstalking for perpetrators, it's important to educate your child about some of their tricks.

The information below is culled from these great resources: newchoicesinc.org, victimsofcrime.org, and haltabuse.org (they have great online safety brochures).

You can be specific when warning your child that cyberstalkers may

- ☐ Try to lure her on dates;
- ☐ Try to engage her in sexting;
- ☐ "Flame" her—which means that the stalker will say something to get her very angry as a hook to keep her engaged in negative conversations;
- ☐ Continuously ask her for her address, birthdate, or cell number;
- ☐ Offer to be her friend;
- ☐ Show her porn photos to entice her;
- ☐ Be both people she knows or doesn't know.

These are things you can do, and teach your child to do, to help decrease potential cyberstalking (from the same sites as noted above):

1. Don't stay logged on; turn off your computer when it's not being used.
2. Assume that everything is public even if you think it's not.
3. When you visit chat rooms or blogs, use a different email from your main one.
4. When choosing your online name, make it gender neutral.

5. Change your password often and make it strong.

6. Change your email address often and only share your personal email with people you know well.

7. Search your own name online to make sure there is nothing suspicious about the content.

8. Save all records you suspect are possible cyberstalking items.

9. Alert your ISP (internet service provider) of any perpetrator actions.

10. **Use the National Center for Victims of Crime for help with all stalking issues (victimsofcrime.org).[1] They list the services available in your particular state.**

I cannot stress enough that no matter what threats may exist through traditional bullying, cyberbullying, cyberstalking, school or neighborhood bullying, or bullying in your home, it is *you* who have the ability to help your child to feel safe and as secure as possible in our shared world. It is with your level of consciousness, kindness, and compassionate expressions of love that you can help to quell your child's cyber concerns if they are, indeed, his.

In my experience as a therapist and educator, I've learned that there's a good and bad way to talk to your child about a cyberbullying event. For example, what do you do if your fourteen-year-old daughter comes to you

---

1 These are applicable for cyberbullying, too.

telling you that one of her friends posted a selfie of her breasts on Facebook and all the kids have it now?

First, be extremely happy that your daughter has shared this with you. It means that she trusts you, she feels it's wrong and wants your confirmation about that, and wonders what, if anything, she should do about it.

Second, compliment her for coming to you with this information and let her know you're proud of her for knowing, or at least suspecting, that her friend has done a dangerous thing.

And third, your daughter's friends are, no doubt, talking about her friend's post. Since she's fourteen, teach her by using questions and when her answers are positive, reinforce them.

The following are two examples of what your response to your child's friend's posted breast selfie might look like. One is positive and one is negative.

Positive Dialogue between Parent and Child

In the following example, the mother and daughter are seated at the kitchen table. The daughter has just shared what her friend has done.

MOM: Are your friends all discussing this?

DAUGHTER: Of course, what do you think!

MOM: I imagined so, but just wanted to be sure. What do you think about it?

DAUGHTER: It seems wrong and I feel bad for her. But you know, Bridgette is known as a slut.

MOM: What do you mean, slut?

DAUGHTER: Well, she lets boys feel her up in the park all the time.

MOM: Her boyfriend or boys?

DAUGHTER: Boys!!! She does other stuff too.

MOM: Like?

DAUGHTER: Do them.

MOM: You mean gives them blowjobs?

DAUGHTER: [Looks shocked as if she cannot imagine her mom would know what that is] Yeah.

MOM: In the park?

DAUGHTER: Yeah.

MOM: [With pained compassion.] Oh no, I feel so sorry for her that she exposes herself like that all over the place. How very sad. Do you think you can be helpful to her in any way?

DAUGHTER: I don't know. How do you mean?

MOM: I mean, let's try to think of some options that might help her. What do you think?

DAUGHTER: I'm not being a tattletale!

MOM: No, of course not. But I'm wondering how you and your friends are dealing with it? I mean do you laugh and gossip about it?

Daughter: Yes, everybody does.

Mom: But you feel it's wrong and I bet some of the others do, too. So, maybe you can start there. What if you suggest to them that you all delete the photo and agree to let it go? And at the same time, perhaps you all can share with Bridgette that you care about her and you think she should delete the photo before it gets worse for her.

Daughter: Hmm, yes, that feels good because Bridgette is my friend and I don't feel good laughing about this stuff with the other kids, even though Bridgette seems proud she did it.

Mom: Do her parents know she's doing these types of things?

Daughter: No.

Mom: How do you think they would deal with it if they knew?

Daughter: They'd be furious. They're very strict and her dad gets violent.

Mom: What do you mean by violent?

Daughter: Once she had a black-and-blue mark from him on her arm.

Mom: This is so upsetting. To think how much Bridgette has already suffered and now she did this and she'll suffer even more. But, you know Ashley, I'm very proud of you. You truly are a good friend to Bridgette by the way you want to help her. I hope your friends will join you in this way of thinking about Bridgette and the danger of posting things she'll regret later.

Daughter: They will. Even though they all shared the photo, I know they think it's wrong.

Mom: Do you think Bridgette can use other help as well?

Daughter: For sure. She's not doing so well in school either, and sometimes the kids in class make fun of her.

Mom: How?

Daughter: Roll their eyes when she says she didn't do the homework . . . again.

Mom: Any other way?

Daughter: Some call her stupid behind her back.

Mom: Does she see the school nurse, guidance counselor, or psychologist?

Daughter: I don't know.

Mom: Sounds like that might help her with what's causing her to make such dangerous decisions.

Daughter: I guess.

Mom: What if you, obviously it would be in the strictest confidence, met with the school psychologist and shared how you are worried about Bridgette and hoped she might be able to keep an eye out for her?

Daughter: Mom, instead, can you phone the school psychologist?

Mom: Yes, but you have the phone option, too. How about it?

Daughter: But if you do it, it will be confidential too, right?

Mom: Right.

Daughter: Please, Mom, you do it.

Mom: Do you want some time to think about making the call?

Daughter: No. I'm too worried Bridgette would find out. Please, mom.

Mom: OK. This can be our secret. Let's hope the school psychologist can help her.

Daughter: Hope so.

Negative Dialogue Between Parent and Child

In an alternative scenario, a very different outcome is likely. For instance, in this next example, the following takes place after the mother enters her daughter's room:

Mom: Hey, Mrs. Rubio told me that Bridgette took a picture of her boobs and put them online! Is that true?

Daughter: I don't know.

Mom: Are you kidding me? She said all the kids know.

DAUGHTER: So?

MOM: So I think that's disgusting. How can you be friends with a girl like that! What a little pig.

DAUGHTER: [Silence.]

MOM: That's all you have to say, nothing?

DAUGHTER: What do you want me to say? You don't even know what Facebook is, and you don't know anything about Bridgette.

MOM: I know enough, and from now on you have to stop being her friend if she's doing things like this.

DAUGHTER: [Searching for a way to make this more real.] How do you know I don't do that, too?

MOM: I know you wouldn't do that. We're not that kind of people. So . . . I see you do know she did it. I thought so!

DAUGHTER: So what!

MOM: So, stay away from that girl.

DAUGHTER: No. She's my friend.

MOM: Well, you could get into trouble with this online stuff. Stay away from her online, too.

DAUGHTER: [Knowing her mom has no idea what she's talking about.] Sure mom.

The mother goes back to the kitchen and the daughter remains in her room at her computer ready to text a friend about how her mom knows about Bridgette. Meanwhile, the only thing this mother expressed was both her lack of empathy and knowledge. By bullying her daughter, in this instance, the mom reinforces the disconnection that already exists between them.

Warning Signs for Cyberbullying

Most organizations, including schools, are addressing the topic of cyberbullying with information that you will find helpful. Use these resources. I particularly recommend a thorough review of warning signs and actions to take regarding cyberbullying by Sameer Hinduja, Ph.D., and Justin W. Patchin, Ph.D., titled, "Cyberbullying: Identification, Prevention, and Response."[2] In this review (found at www.cyberbullying.us), you'll find up-to-date data on cyberbullying and suggested steps for dealing with cyberbullying whether your child is the perpetrator or the victim.

Following are warning signs quoted from Dr. Hinduja and Dr. Patchin's work.

A Child May Be a Target of Cyberbullying If He or She

☐ Unexpectedly stops using her device;

☐ Appears nervous or jumpy when using her device(s).

---

[2] Hinduja, Sameer, Justin Patchin. "Cyberbullying Identification, Prevention, and Response." *Cyberbullying Research Center*, cyberbullying.org. 2014.

- ☐ Appears uneasy about going to school or outside in general;
- ☐ Appears angry, depressed, or frustrated after going online (including gaming);
- ☐ Is oversleeping or not sleeping enough;
- ☐ Becomes abnormally withdrawn from usual friends and family members;
- ☐ Shows increase or decrease in eating;
- ☐ Seems regularly depressed;
- ☐ Makes passing statements about suicide or the meaninglessness of life;
- ☐ Loses interest in the things that mattered most to her;
- ☐ Avoids discussions about what she is doing online;
- ☐ Frequently calls or texts from school requesting to go home ill;
- ☐ Wants to spend much more time with parents rather than peers;
- ☐ Becomes unusually secretive, especially when it comes to online activities.[3]

---

3 Ibid.

A Child May Be Cyberbullying Others If He or She

- ☐ Quickly switches screens or hides his device(s) when you are close by;
- ☐ Uses his device at all hours of day or night;
- ☐ Gets unusually upset if he can't use his device(s);
- ☐ Laughs excessively while using his device(s) and won't show what is so funny;
- ☐ Avoids discussions about what he's doing online;
- ☐ Seems to be using multiple online accounts or an account that is not his own;
- ☐ Is dealing with increased behavioral issues or disciplinary actions at school (or elsewhere);
- ☐ Appears overly concerned with popularity or continued presence in a particular social circle or status level;
- ☐ Demonstrates increasing insensitivity or callousness toward other teens;
- ☐ Starts to hang out with the "wrong" crowd;
- ☐ Demonstrates violent tendencies;
- ☐ Appears overly conceited as to technological skills and abilities;
- ☐ Your parent-child relationship is deteriorating.

These same authors[4] offer ten things parents can do when their child is cyberbullied:

---

4 Ibid.

1. Make sure your child feels safe.
2. Talk with and listen to your child.
3. Collect evidence.
4. Work with the school.
5. Refrain from contacting the parents of the bully.
6. Contact the content provider.
7. Contact the police when physical threats are involved.
8. If the bullying is based on race, sex, or disability, contact the Office of Civil Rights, U.S. Department of Education.
9. If necessary, seek counseling.
10. Implement measures to prevent cyberbullying from recurring.

For more extensive suggestions and further delineations of these ten tips please see www.cyberbullying.us. Also skim through "Cyberbullying Legislation and Case Law," which you will find on the same site.

A Word about Suicide Risk Factors

As we've seen, one of the warning signs that suggest your child might be a target of cyberbullying, as well as other forms of bullying, is that she makes passing statements about suicide or general comments about the meaninglessness of life. Common responses about the meaninglessness of life which are not one-offs but are patterns:

1. I don't know why I should even bother. Nobody cares anyway.
2. Repeated use of "uh huh" to just blow you off.
3. I don't care.
4. I'm not going; they don't like me.
5. Not interested in any stupid games.
6. Don't ask me anything. I don't want to talk.
7. No response to rewards or punishments.
8. Not tending to self-care and never discussing it, just saying, "I don't care if I wash my hair, so why should you?"

Because it's so important, I'm adding the following information about possible suicidal risk elements:[5]

- ☐ History of depression (or other serious mental illness);
- ☐ History of or active use of alcohol or drug abuse;
- ☐ Recent stressful or traumatic life event or history of trauma;
- ☐ History of previous suicide attempts;
- ☐ Family history of suicide;

---

5 *American Foundation for Suicide Prevention*, American Foundation for Suicide Prevention, www.afsp.org.

- ☐ Suicide occurrences within social circles;
- ☐ Gay, lesbian, bisexual, and transgender youth are more prone to suicide attempts than their straight peers.

What You Can Do If You Suspect Your Child May Be Having Suicidal Thoughts[6]

1. Encourage communication with you.
2. Show your concern and love.
3. Be nonjudgmental regarding the incidents and feelings he shares.
4. Never trivialize your child's concerns.
5. If your child is having trouble sharing with you, suggest he confide in a trusted relative, friend, or family doctor with whom he has a good relationship. A trusted religious leader could also be helpful, as could a trusted camp or school counselor.
6. Don't be afraid to ask your child if he's contemplated suicide.
7. If you can get him to, have him promise not to take that action.
8. If you can get him to, have him refrain from alcohol and drugs.

---

[6] Ibid.

9. Suggest professional treatment—the school psychologist, a local therapist referred to you by your doctor, a therapist suggested to you by word of mouth or from the local hospital—and make sure he gets there. Be certain the professional you choose is experienced with children at risk for suicide.

10. If you become concerned in between your child's appointments with his counselor, contact the professional yourself with your worries and ask that person for proper next steps.

11. If you do suspect your child is at imminent risk, take your child to the nearest hospital emergency room or call 911.

Will My Child Lose Her Social Skills Because of So Much Time Spent Online?

Many parents, as well as some professionals, bemoan the fact that children are not really learning to communicate properly because they are always online. They fear children might be limiting their social skills development because they are constantly on devices.

I don't agree. They are not communicating with their devices, they're communicating with others using devices. Clearly, they use their devices for good, bad, and ugly experiences, but they are communicating. They are communicating as children always have, intensely and obsessively, just as they do at lunchtime, in the schoolyard, at the local yogurt shop, or walking to and from school.

They are utilizing more avenues of communication, but they are also comparing notes just as older folks did during their intense, obsessive phone calling when they were kids.

Sometimes children are in small groups discussing what a friend has discovered online; sometimes they are sharing music or a new fashion item that has just come out. Or they are sharing who said what to whom, and how so-and-so reacted. Other times they are sharing texts, tweets or an email someone has just sent. They may frequently compare research they've found for homework assignments.

Is there bullying and cyberbullying to address? Of course! And, as mentioned above, the cyber part of bullying adds pitfalls and requires more parental vigilance. But remember, intervention becomes successful based upon the nature of the connection of each parent with each child (and available support services).

The most important remedies for parental non-bullying, cyber or other, require you to be as bi-conscious as humanly possible on any given day in any particular moment. Your expanding consciousness will allow you to love your child more precisely, fully, and satisfyingly. This brings us to a tool which will enhance your efforts—Time In.

CHAPTER FIVE

Time In: A New Parenting Tool

*"Don't spend time beating on a wall,
hoping to transform it into a door."*

— Coco Chanel
(née Gabrielle Bonheur, 1883–1971)

"Jeez, I could really use a time out!"

We often say this just prior to booking a long overdue vacation or telling a friend we've "had it up to here" with our bosses, husbands, wives or kids. It's also frequently used as a discipline tool by parents, teachers, love partners, and childcare workers. Many of us do, in fact, take time outs when we've hit our last-straw moments, and find them very helpful as a way to gain back control we feel we somehow have lost.

We're so accustomed to sending ourselves and others for time outs, we miss the fact that what we really need is more "Time In." We need to change our focus from escape to engagement so we can more easily and more authentically connect with our children. We need to switch from frustrated rejection and withdrawal to more regular acceptance and engagement with them—in other words, we need fewer time outs and more Time Ins.

What is Time In?

As noted in chapter 1, Time In is a self-esteem enhancing tool for both children and adults built on the premise that the more you are able to control and manage your attitudes and behaviors, the stronger and better you will feel about yourself. And the stronger and better you feel about yourself, the better you will treat others.

Most importantly, Time In is a tool to help you create a non-bullying way of life, and it is a reminder that empathy and compassion for yourself and for your child requires that you take the time necessary to pay attention to the nuances of emotional realities.

Further, Time In requires focusing your non-judgmental attention on establishing and nurturing positive emotional, physical, mental, and social connections every chance you get. It's the space in which you consciously intend to accept and deliver positive actions and reactions. Its goal, as noted above, is to help you create non-bullying environments for all aspects of your child's life through fostering compassionate interpersonal connections.

In *your* heart and mind lie the most powerful tools we have for remitting bullying in our society. Without question, *you* have this power. Use all the tools available to you to deliver the best of you to your child. The Eight-Step Parenting Method of self-examination and the Time In tool will help you reach that goal.

I know it is not easy to maintain the non-bullying, compassionate kind of parental vigilance that I've described earlier. And, because of that, one can tend to slide into automatic, impulsive reactions that foster discord and/or violence in the sphere of relationships with your child. However, even just *remembering* that Time In requires an embracing, non-judgmental state of mind will help you remain the conscious adult I know you want to be; the one who is able to confidently de-escalate a potentially destructive drama with his child (such as delineated in chapter 3, The Eight-Step Parenting Method).

There are so many times that a Time In would better serve than a time out to calm an out-of-control child or situation. I can recall so many occasions when a teacher removed a child from the classroom and when I later followed up and asked why was the child removed, the answer often was, "I had just had it up to here with that kid."

I was struck by the fact that the focus of the teacher's explanation was the teacher's need, not the child's. In pursuit of the real reason for ejecting the child from the classroom, what I inevitably found was that too little time had been paid to the child's real needs long before the desire to throw him out of the classroom occurred.

In my practice I ask parents relatively the same question when I inquire why they had ordered a particular time out.

"I just had had enough," is often the answer. Again, the focus of the statement is on the parent's need, not the child's. When I examine what it is the parent has had enough of, invariably it is the anger, unhappiness, stubbornness, and any other displeasing and destructive behaviors the child is manifesting. How the child gets to those destructive behaviors is often the result of a sequence of past (old or new) emotional abandonments by the parent.

> A child's peak level of frustration is usually when a parent often reaches his own desperation level.

What I've discovered is that in many of these experiences, a child's needs have gone unanswered for so long, she can't take it anymore and, thus, acts out her frustration in negative ways. A child's peak level of frustration is usually when a parent often reaches his own desperation level. And since parents, often at their desperation level, have no idea what the real problem is or how to fix it, they send the child for a time out. In this type of scenario, the burden of gaining control is placed on the child. It's she who is made to feel guilty and wrong about what she's feeling.

What would be more helpful is for the parent to accept responsibility for his own frustrations earlier, in an attempt to preempt the escalation of the child's frustrations and subsequent non-compliance. The key question for the parent to ask himself is, "When did I first notice the slightest change in my child's countenance and what were my reactions to that?" If you start your self-questioning backward from the final horrible level of a blow-up situation, and answer honestly, you will get to the root cause (trigger event or tone) of your child's meltdown, which triggered your escalating frustration levels and had you sending him for a time out.

Now for the requirements for successful use of Time Ins. Label *Time Ins*, Time Ins, so all get accustomed to the meaning of the tag, Time In as representing *a specific time for compassionate and safe interactions.*

The Essential Characteristics of a Time In

1. Empathy and compassion are the guiding principles for interactions.

2. Whatever time is needed to hear and be heard is given.

3. a. Examining your unconscious intentions is expected as part of your responsibility for assuring the best Time Ins possible.

   b. Self-questions are *required* for Time Ins. For example,

   "Am I able to be kind now?"

   "Do I feel loving?"

   "Did I cause him pain? And if I did, can I genuinely apologize for it?"

   "Am I suffering in silence about something while acting grumpy?"

   "Am I being a bully or am I being my loving, wonderful, caring self?"

   "Am I filled with impatience, resentment, jealousy, and anger right now? If I am, why is that? What should I do to change it?"

4. Kindness rules in a Time In. It must feel genuine to you. If it does, it will feel genuine to your child, too.

5. Self-talk recommendation for Time In use:

a. "I have both the time and patience to give and receive what is needed for Time In success."

   b. No matter what bully-victim scenario is going on, say to yourself:

   "I have the tools to deal with this."

   "The answers are within me."

   "Making change is within my power."

   "I am quite capable of being a bi-conscious person."

6. Consciously focus on the good in your life, no matter how tiny that good may be on a given day. I know this is sometimes very hard, but try, since it will help balance some possible lingering negativity.

7. Judge, but don't be judgmental. This is difficult for some to understand and accomplish, so I will expand on it here. The truth is that we judge all the time. There is zero wrong with it. For example, "I prefer string beans to peas." We evaluate everything and we're supposed to; otherwise how would we ever make decisions? Just don't make your judgments (choices) in a condescending, judgmental manner. There is no reason to insult peas because you prefer string beans!

Where to Use Time In

Time In is a highly flexible tool since it can be used anytime and anywhere. You may want to establish a Time In space as a particular room to be used for processing difficult scenarios. But it can be set up wherever you are able to reflect the characteristics of a Time In as outlined above, and respect the rules for Time In as they are outlined below. Just make certain that you label the time as a Time In, so your child (or others) knows it is an emotionally protected event.

Again, if physical space is limited, you can designate any area that offers privacy as your Time In Space. If you happen to be outside and need to use a Time In, pick a relatively private spot that will support your Time In mission. Once you do, then focus so intently on your child that no ancillary noise will exist for you. When you do that, it won't exist for your child either.

For example, suppose you're at the park with your child and she's refusing to play with the other children. You've tried encouraging her to play with the others but no, she keeps walking around with her head down, all by herself. If this type of scenario is a pattern and you've tried Time Ins for a while, as well as other techniques for changing behavior, consider seeking professional help.

If, however, this isn't a pattern of behavior yet, instead of continuing to focus on the playground and the other children, gently take your daughter's hand and select a private, quiet spot away from the other kids and parents. Sit down together and search for the real reasons for your child's withdrawal from playing with her friends at the playground.

This, of course, assumes you follow the rules and expectations for Time In use.

Rules for Time Ins

1. The most important rule is the one we know as the Golden Rule. Hillel the Elder (c.100 BCE) wrote, "That which is hateful to you, do not do to your fellow." In other words "Treat people the way you wish they'd treat you." Easy enough to state, hard to do.

2. Be humble.

3. *Assume* you'll be able to give what is needed. If you feel, *for any reason,* that you can't, STOP. BREATHE. REVIEW your Eight-Step Parenting Method. Then, push through as best you can and your child will *feel your purity of intent* and you will find, in that change of your energy, that success more likely will follow. If you still feel you can't give what is needed, ask for help.

4. No one is to be judged as being a bad person for anything. Your children will make mistakes, some small, some large, but no matter what type of mistake is brought to the Time In, the child is to be received with empathy and compassion.

5. Judge the behaviors of the child, not the child! Some actions are wrong, but when addressed with kindness they are more easily corrected. Always without judgment, hear the child's feelings first and then

correct her behaviors. In the Time In Space, kindness is the underpinning of all actions. Remember Buddha's great words, *"When words are both true and kind, they can change the world."* Words spoken without judgment will help change your child's behaviors. No question about it.

6. If a Time In is requested, give it gladly. If you can't do it right away, and the issue *isn't severe,* and the reason you can't do it a simply a logistical one, set a time and place that will work better. But transmit your authentic willingness to hear whatever the issue is. *This assumes you've set a pattern of keeping your word.*

7. No matter how awful you feel your child's behavior has been, make it your mission to hear his story.

8. Don't interrupt your child (or other) as he is talking unless he's breaking a Time In rule.

9. Acknowledge that you've heard what your child (or other) wants you to hear by *expressing* that you understand his feeling and his perceptions of an event or circumstance. Empathize with his feelings, then offer your well-thought-out and compassionate responses *for* him. Make sure that the issue of the moment is resolved or that there is a plan in place for its resolution that all involved are comfortable with.

10. Authentically apologize if apologizing is what is needed.

11. Say thank you when you've been heard. Say thank you to your child for sharing his truths even if they were hard to hear.

12. Words may not be used as weapons. Therefore, make sure you check for any negative attitude before you speak.

13. Note that the difference between a chat and a Time In is that there are rules for a Time In that require empathy, compassion, and kindness. Embracing the ritual for a Time In enhances awareness for responsible emotional, social, intellectual, and physical behaviors.

    In time, Time In Rules for enhancing your positive interactions with your child (and others) will be absorbed into your daily life. And with that truth realized, your bully-victim behaviors will diminish.

When Should Parents Use Time Ins

Parents should use Time Ins when they detect that their child is emotionally, physically, socially, or mentally *off*. Parents know that if their child is hungry, she'll act up. Once that's obvious, they know to feed her. A Time In creates the chance to expand your considerations to the things that could possibly set your child's equilibrium *off*, other than the obvious physical ones like hunger, thirst, or fatigue. Look for hurts that may stem from your child's interactions with others or a disappointment that may have recently occurred. Then, call for a Time In to explore the things that might be causing the hurts and provide the necessary antidotes.

For example, a ten-year-old boy, Harlan, who is usually a happy, energetic boy, has been quiet and withdrawn since he came home from school. He usually gets to his homework right after a snack but hasn't done that on this particular day. Instead, he starts to play his flute. After fifteen minutes you remind him to get to his homework so you can both read together later. He complies and starts his homework, but you notice he's doing it in slow motion and slumping in his chair. Perfect time for a Time In.

I expand this example here since the reason for this boy's sad affect is, unfortunately, not that uncommon. When the mom in this illustration explored the reason for Harlan's loss of energy, she discovered he had been bullied in gym because he is terrible at sports. Some other boys called him sissy and fag and kept snickering at him as they whispered among themselves while staring at him.

Harlan is a delicate boy and some would say effeminate. Although this mom is unquestionably non-judgmental, her heart breaks to know he is not like most of the boys his age. She knows that many adults still can't accept differences in sexual or gender preferences and, therefore, their children mimic their prejudices. She's worried that Harlan will have to navigate a rocky road.

She loves Harlan dearly, no matter what his future gender or sexual inclinations may be. Her first response, therefore, is to let him know how awful that experience must have felt and how sad it is those boys are so unkind. Her focus in this Time In discussion is on Harlan's wonderful uniqueness and his many superior talents for a boy his age. She is able to help him understand that it is the other boys' fear of differences that make them act so mean.

Harlan knows enough to know what the meanings of homosexuality and transgender are.

"Do you think I'm gay?" he asks his mom.

She is wonderfully honest.

"I don't know, but if you are that would be fine with me. As long as you're a happy boy and become a happy adult who loves whatever you do and whomever you choose, that's totally fine. Right now your job is to accept your many gifts and know how much you are loved and appreciated just because you're you. Time will let us know the rest, so never forget you are lovable and fine just the way you are."

After a few more minutes of hugging and wiping tears, Harlan began his homework in his usual confident way as his mom wrapped him in the brightest light her mind could possibly send his way.

You can also use a Time In when you're proud of something your child did or didn't do.

For example, your child followed a house rule consistently for a week after having not complied with that rule for a month prior. Or, you observed that your child didn't join in with the other children who were making fun of another child. The use of Time Ins for positive reinforcement of the qualities you desire for your children will reinforce them.

Let Time In be a space that helps you to remember what I call the **Four C's**. They are: **C**entered, **C**alm, **C**ompassionate, and with **C**alibrated intentions. These **C's** will help you focus on how best to present yourself in interactions.

Use Time Ins regularly, as they encourage you to model appropriate empathetic and compassionate behaviors. Your consistency of empathy and compassion will encourage your child to ask for Time Ins since they offer assured loving and accepting experiences. The Time In experiences become a wonderful way for your child to learn to monitor her emotional, physical, social, and mental life, as well as to take responsibility for her behaviors, especially for when she senses that she's *losing it*.

I've found that parents, in time, incorporate the Time In rules and characteristics for their family meetings, and that has proven helpful for them.

It always delights me when one child in one family receives attention in a new way and that new way leaves that one child feeling more loved, happier, and more confident. As well, the satisfaction I see in one parent's heart when she successfully uses a new parenting tool and grows more confident as a parent is a similar delight.

Time Ins versus Time Outs

If, you're wonderfully bi-conscious regarding parenting and deliver your instructions for time outs with calm, certainty, empathy, and compassion, your child will understand and feel comfortable with your directives. She'll accept time outs more happily than if you demand them in an angry, humiliating, and rejecting tone. Even if your daughter fights you about the time out, she knows deep down if it feels right, even if she can't admit or articulate that at the time.

Conversely, when you use time outs angrily and frequently, they become punishments that lose their potency and purpose as instruments of teaching. The result is more than just the continuation of the out-of-control behaviors of the moment, they become a long-lasting destruction of emotional trust between you and your child.

A broken emotional bond doesn't depend solely on your repeated use of time outs. Emotional trust can also be worn down by all the seemingly little things that come prior to a need for a time out.

The Little Things

Everything is built from little things and little things are powerful. One caring call can lighten a lonely heart. One surprise gift to a child of any age can help solidify his hope that life offers good things. A tiny sperm found its tiny egg, and here we are, alive.

It is often the seemingly little things that shape the tenor of your days. Pay attention to them, since how you deal with all the little things influences not only your child's daily life but her future life as well. A precisely delivered empathic comment will help foster a loving connection between you and your child; an unconsciously driven unkind comment can foster feelings in your child of confusion and emotional betrayal. The Little Things that are often overlooked as unimportant, and that I refer to here, are the impulsive, emotionally inaccurate, and unconscious attempts to meet a child's needs that she experiences as emotional betrayals.

When incidents of emotional betrayal accrue, your child's trust in you as a reliable emotional resource is eroded. This is how communication schisms grow between you and your child—little thing by little thing, moment to moment, day by day, year by year. In the time you don't take to "really" hear your child's heart and respond in a way that directly answers his need, you are emotionally abandoning him. He begins to feel lonely and helpless, and his self-esteem shrinks. These precious, lost moments of perceiving the true, actual needs of your child are the breeding grounds for him to become a victim or a bully.

> . . . an unconsciously driven unkind comment can foster feelings in your child of confusion and emotional betrayal.

Time Out Experienced as Emotional Betrayal

The following is a composite example from my practice. It is of a time out that feeds a child's feelings of emotional betrayal and reinforces the schism of trust between parent and child.

Two children were fighting. Barbara is eight years old and Larry is five years old. Their mom came into the room in which the children were fighting since their screaming was at a very high pitch.

"Larry is trying to take away my toy," Barbara told her mom.

"That's my toy," Larry said, "Barbara stole it from me and I'm just trying to get it back."

"Give Barbara back the toy," the mom told Larry.

"That's not fair, she took it from me," Larry protested.

"You're whining and acting like a baby, Larry," Mom screamed, "so go to your room for a time out. Not another word out of your mouth!"

"Why won't you listen to me?" Larry sobbed, "She took it from me and it's mine and I just want it back, momma, please."

"I told you not another word. Go to your room for a time out, and if I hear any more screaming from you it will be a longer time out. Just go and shut up."

Crying, defeated, and forlorn Larry goes to his room.

Poor Larry. He wasn't given a chance to tell his side of things and, on top of that unfair treatment, he gets a time out for what he feels is an injustice to him. This mother settled the fight with seeming expedience—sending Larry to his room for a time out. What she actually achieved was erosion in trust and additional pain for Larry, Barbara, and herself. None of them, in this scenario, know what each other's truth is.

The background for the mother in this illustration will shed some light on her quick, unconscious use of a time out. The mom not only feels harried at her job, but she has been totally unsupported by her husband as far as parenting is concerned. He often sits in the same room where a fight is going on and takes no action with his children to resolve it. None.

"Don't you see what is going on here?" she'll say to her husband.

"Oh, yeah," he replies and does nothing to help. Instead he makes a phone call to his secretary just to check in.

It's easy to understand and have compassion for this mom since she's alone and responsible for most of the parenting responsibilities for both Barbara and Larry. It's also easy to appreciate how the use of the time out is a reflection of this mom's stretched level of patience. The result of that lack of patience becomes an emotional betrayal to all involved in this particular drama.

Because this mom loves her children very much, reacting inappropriately to her children in their time of need pained her to the point that she knew she needed help. I'm happy to report, therefore, that this mother, her children, and the father are doing much better since the mother stepped into my office a few years ago.

The Barbara and Larry Example Revisited

Here's a rewind picture of how the mom and her two children would play out their conflict after some therapeutic counseling about Time Ins.

A sister and brother are fighting. Barbara is eight years old and Larry is five. Their mom comes into the room where the children are fighting since their screaming is at a very high pitch and didn't sound friendly.

"Larry is trying to take my toy and won't let it go," Barbara tells her mom.

"It's really my toy and Barbara stole it and I'm just trying to get it back," Larry tells her mom.

"Oh my goodness, my two angels are so upset!" Mom says, "We need a Time In—all of us. And that includes poor Annabelle, [stuffed alligator] who is being pulled apart; I can hear her crying. First, let me hold Annabelle until we settle this issue between you two. Does either of you need a tissue, glass of water, or other stuffed animal to hold for our Time In?

"No," Barbara and Larry both reply.

"Who wants to be the first one to tell me what happened?"

"Me! Me!" both children cry.

"OK. Since you both want to start, I'll toss a coin for who tells first. Heads is Larry, tails is Barbara."

"No," Barbara says, "I want heads."

"Why? Both have equal chance of landing heads up."

"It's my favorite."

"Oh . . . I didn't know that."

"She just wants to tell first, heads comes first!" Larry says.

"Hmm. Larry, do you care if you have heads or tails?"

"Yes, heads is my favorite, too."

"Wow, I can't believe it. I didn't know my two children both loved heads so much more than tails. Here's what we'll do. We'll use a dice. Each of you, pick a number from one to six and write it down on a piece of paper. The one whose number rolls up first gets to be the first one to tell me the story of what happened with Annabelle.

"OK," both children say.

"Ok, Barbara, your number came up first, so tell me what happened from your point of view."

"Larry was trying to take my toy from me."

"Now, Larry, you tell me what happened from your point of view."

"Barbara stole Annabelle from me. Annabelle is mine, not hers."

"But the other day he said I could have her."

"Larry, did you tell Barbara she could have Annabelle?"

"I said she could play with her. I didn't say she could *have* her.

"Barbara, did you know Larry only lent Annabelle to you?"

"No. He said I could have her. Then, today, when I was in the middle of playing with Annabelle, that's when he said it was only for lend."

"Oh, I get it."

"What?" both asked.

"Looks like Larry changed his mind. He didn't know how to ask you if it was OK with you that he changed his mind about Annabelle, so he did the wrong thing by trying to just take her back."

"Right, I didn't steal her."

"Larry," Mom asked, "why did you give Annabelle to Barbara the other day when you only meant to lend her to Barbara?"

"I don't know. I didn't mean to; I love her, she's my favorite animal."

Barbara asks, "So, is Annabelle mine?"

"It seems Larry did give Annabelle to you; so, yes. But it looks like Larry made a mistake, and we'll try to figure out why in our separate Time In time. Larry, do you want to apologize to Barbara for grabbing Annabelle away from her instead of discussing it?"

"OK, sorry Barbara."

"Barbara, anything you might want to say to Larry about the hitting and kicking?"

"Yes, I should have asked for a Time In with you and Larry instead of continuing the fight."

"Forget anything?"

"Oh yeah . . . Sorry, Larry. And . . . [A thinking pause occurs here] I'll let you play with Annabelle sometimes."

"Wow, that is so sweet of you, Barbara, to hear that Larry feels so badly about his mistake that you want to share Annabelle with him. I am so proud of you for caring about how Larry feels."

"I'll let you play with Coconut if you want," Larry enthusiastically says to Barbara.

"OK."

"I'm proud of both of you. Oh, and Barbara, if you want a special Time In with me about this we can set that up, too."

"No, I'm OK, mom."

Time spent in a Time In solidifies emotional bonds. Using the example above of a positive Time In session with Barbara and Larry, here are some of its positive outcomes:

1. Larry's trust in his mom to emotionally take care of him is solidified.

2. Larry's trust that things will be fair, even if he made a mistake, is solidified.

3. Larry's trust in his sister is solidified.

4. Larry is relieved of carrying the guilt of lying.

5. Barbara's trust in her mother to be fair is solidified.

6. Barbara's trust that her mom cares enough to find out the truth is solidified.
7. Barbara is relieved of carrying guilt about hitting and kicking which she knows is wrong.
8. The mom feels good about herself since she solved a problem with kindness, compassion, and fairness.
9. The emotional bond between the mother and her children is solidified.

The same types of positive outcomes can be yours when you incorporate the proper use of Time Ins.

Here's a fun way for parents to remember their solemn commitments to their children:

> We the people who have children, in order to form more perfect unions with them, establish justice for and with them, insure domestic tranquility, provide for their defense, promote their general welfare, and secure our blessings of liberty for ourselves and our posterity, do ordain and establish this commitment to the Four C's of interacting with our children: remain Centered, Calm, Compassionate and proceed with Calibrated Intentions.

We can try . . . and that's a big thing.

CHAPTER SIX

The Power of Forgiving

"Power is of two kinds. One is obtained by the fear of punishment and the other by acts of love. Power based on love is a thousand times more effective and permanent than the one derived from fear of punishment."

—MAHATMA GANDHI (1869–1948)

President Obama, in his June 27, 2015, eulogy for Clementa C. Pinckney—who was killed at Emanuel African Methodist Episcopal Church in Charleston, South Carolina, by a man filled with hatred—shared his understanding of Rev. Pinckney's way of thinking. He said,

> *He understood that justice grows out of recognition of ourselves in each other. That my liberty depends on you being free, too. That history can't be a sword to justify injustice, or a shield against progress, but*

> *must be a manual for how to avoid repeating the mistakes of the past—how to break the cycle.*

He further quoted the Pulitzer Prize winning author "Marilyn Robinson describing

> *'that reservoir of goodness, beyond, and of another kind, that we are able to do for each other in the ordinary cause of things. That reservoir of goodness. If we can find that grace, anything is possible. If we can tap that grace, everything can change.'"*

We can only find that grace by recognizing in ourselves not just the good, but the bad and the ugly, too. Accepting that imperfect human condition in others and forgiving them their trespasses as we forgive our own is another profound maxim in action.

> . . . *the unconscious, and your relationship with it, influences your life forcefully.*

Real forgiving is hard. Genuine forgiveness is difficult unless you understand the essential fact that the unconscious, and your relationship with it, influences your life forcefully. The forgiveness that priests, rabbis, ministers, or imams offer you will never have as much power for your personal growth, and for the development of your soul, as the forgiveness you're able to find within yourself for yourself.

If you've grown comfortable with forgiving, it implies you have accepted that when it comes to bullying and victimhood, you may be the cause as well as the cure. The more you know the origins of your own pains, the more you'll be able to know bullies and victims as being vulnerable to similar causes of pain. Out of that knowledge of your shared humanity, you'll be able to respond to bullies with appropriate, and more consciously chosen, emotional and empathic care.

You can become a hero or heroine of forgiveness when you face your fears, open the door to your demons, and wrestle with them until you've escaped their hold on you. What appears clear to me from my work with many and various types and ages of bullies and victims is that resistance to taking responsibility for bullying begins with our unawareness that we're all bi-conscious beings.

It is my contention that learning to be bi-conscious is both a societal and personal obligation. It behooves us all, and especially those of us who consistently interact with children—including parents, school personnel, nannies, therapists, social workers, medical personnel, housekeepers, paraprofessionals, religious teachers, and athletic coaches—to examine in fine detail what the impact of our own unconscious life is on everyone whom we so profoundly effect.

Some professionals, as well as lay writers, suggest that when we refer to children's behavior, we should be very careful not to label the everyday mean and hurtful acts they do as bullying. They suggest, rather, that we view these acts as simply the common, everyday dramas that kids need to experience as part of their growing up. They consider small mean acts, such as taunting, snide remarks, and leaving children out of a game, fine fodder that fosters children's emotional and social growth.

I agree that growing stronger through adversity can bring beneficial rewards to children. There's no dearth of opportunity to do so as life unfolds. But I would caution us not to make too light of these little dramas, as they often become the foundations for troubling patterns of bullying to develop. Let's not use our knowledge of the possibility of growth through adversity to avoid taking necessary actions to deter bullying.

Nipping little mean acts early—hurtful taunts, pokes, sarcastic remarks, shunning, rejection, and undercurrents of stereotypical judgments—must be seen as an essential part of bully prevention, not as impediments to a child's ability to handle adversity on his own.

Your evaluations of when and how to intercede or not with children will be enhanced by living and using the suggestions outlined in this book.

This is, indeed, a big challenge. But the challenge to embrace our unconscious life with as much vigor and passion as we have invested in exploring our conscious one, is a pursuit our human species needs to follow in order to combat the violent forces present in our world. It's in your hands. You are the saviors. Look inside and you will find your strengths.

You, I, all of us, have the power to change the world. It happens one person by one person, little thing by little thing. Let's use our new powers wisely and kindly and have tons of fun doing it.

Only Connect.

Try again.

Celebrate.

Let's not use our knowledge of the possibility of growth through adversity to avoid taking necessary actions to deter bullying.

HELPFUL RESOURCES

Intervention Strategies

Anthony, Michelle. *Little Girls Can Be Mean.* St. Martin's Griffin, 2010.

Armstrong, Karen. *Twelve Steps To A Compassionate Life.* First Anchor Books, 2011.

Aron, Elaine N. *The Highly Sensitive Person.* Three Rivers Press, 1996

Aron, Elaine N. *The Highly Sensitive Child.* Three Rivers Press, 2002.

Bazelon, Emily. *Sticks and Stones.* Random House, 2013.

Beane, Allan. *Bullying Prevention for Schools.* Jossey-Bass, 2009.

Brown, Brené, *The Gifts of Imperfection.* Hazelden, 2010.

Dosani, Sabina. *Bullying* (52 Brilliant Ideas). Infinite Ideas Trade: Amazon, 2008.

Eisler, Riane. *The Power of Partnership.* New World Library, 2002.

Engel, Beverly. *Healing Your Emotional Self.* John Wiley, 2007.

Espelage, Dorothy L., Susan Swearer (Editors). *Bullying in North American Schools* [Paperback]. Rutledge, 2010.

Gottman, John, Joan Declaire. *Raising An Emotionally Intelligent Child.* Simon & Schuster Paperbacks, 1997.

Haber, Joel, Jenna Glatzer. *Bullyproof Your Child for Life.* The Penguin Group, 2007.

Horn, Sam. *Take The Bully By the Horns.* St. Martin's Press, 2002.

Jung, C.G. *The Practice of Psychotherapy.* Collected Works: Vol.16. Princeton University Press, 1954.

LeCroy, Craig Winston, Joyce Elizabeth Mann. *Handbook of Prevention and Intervention Programs for Adolescent Girls.* Wiley, 2007

Lohmann, Raychelle Cassada, Julia V. Taylor, *The Bullying Workbook for Teens: Activities to Help You Deal with Social Aggression and Cyberbullying.* Instant Help, 20013.

Ludwig, Trudy, Abigail Marble (Illustrator). *My Secret Bully.* Tricycle Press, 2005

Ludwig, Trudy, Adam Gustavson (Illustrator). *Just Kidding.* Tricycle Press, 2006.

Ludwig, Trudy, Beth Adams. *Confessions of a Former Bully.* Dragonfly Books, 2012.

Olweus, Dan. *Bullying at School: What we know and what we can do.* Wiley, 1993.

Phelan, Thomas W. *1-2-3 Magic.* ParentMagic, Inc. 2014.

Rigby, Ken. *Bullying in Schools and what we can do about it.* Jessica Kingsley Publishers, 1997.

Roberts Jr., Walter B. *Bullying From Both Sides.* Corwin Press, 2006.

Roberts Jr., Walter B. *Working With Parents of Bullies and Victims.* Corwin Press, 2008.

Siegel, Daniel J., Mary Hartzell. *Parenting from Inside Out.* Tarcher/Penguin, 2004.

Siegel, Daniel. *The Mindful Therapist.* W.W. Norton & Company, 2010.

Siegel, Daniel J., Tina Payne Bryson. *The Whole-Brain Child.* Bantam Books Trade Paperback Edition, 2012.

Siegel, Daniel, Tina Payne Bryson. *No Drama Discipline.* Bantam, 2014.

Smith, Peter, Debra Pepler, Ken Rigby. *Bullying in Schools: How Successful Can Interventions Be?* [Paperback]. Cambridge University Press, 2004.

Sornson, Bob, Maria Dismondy. *The Juice Box Bully: Empowering Kids to Stand Up for Others.* Early Learning Foundation, 2010.

Swearer, Susan M., Dorothy L. Espelage, Scott A. Napolitano. *Bullying Prevention and Intervention:*

Realistic Strategies for Schools, Practical Intervention in Schools series. The Guilford Press, 2009.

Bullying, Cultural, and Societal Observations

Angelou, Maya. *I Know why the Caged Bird Sings.* Ballantine Books, 2009.

Bazelon, Emily. *Sticks and Stones.* Random House, 2013.

Chödrön, Pema. *The Compassion Book.* Shambhala, 2017.

Coloroso, B. *The bully, the bullied and the bystander: Breaking the cycle of violence.* Collins Updated Edition, 2008.

Dervin, Dan, *2010: The Year of the Bully.* The Journal of Psychohistory, 2010.

Eisler, Riane. *The Chalice & The Blade.* HarperCollins, 1988.

Eisler, Riane. *Tomorrow's Children.* Westview Press, 2000.

Gaskell, G. A. *Dictionary of All Scriptures And Myths.* Julian Press, 1960.

Hillman, James. *The Soul's Code – In Search of Character and Calling.* Grand Central Publishing, 1996.

Holland, Julie. *Medicating Women's Feelings.* New York Times Article: March1, 2015.

Jung, C.G. *Man and His Symbols.* Dell, 1968.

Jung, C.G. Collected Works, *The Archetypes and the Collective Unconscious.* Princeton University Press: Vol. 9.1, 1968.

Jung, *C.G. Jung Speaking.* Princeton University Press, 1977.

Kevorkian, Meline, Robin D'Antona. *101 Facts about Bullying: What Everyone Should Know.* R& L Education: 50756th Edition, August 15, 2008.

Kuklin, Susan. *Beyond Magenta: Transgender Teens Speak Out.* Candlewick, 2015.

Levy, Ariel. *the rules do not apply.* Random House, 2017.

Mehta, Jal. *The Allure of Order.* Oxford University Press, 2013.

Palmer, Helen. *Inner Knowing.* J. Tarcher/Putnam, 1998.

Randall, Lisa. *Knocking On Heaven's Door.* HarperCollins Publishers, 2011.

Sorensen, Michael. *I Hear You: The Surprisingly Simple Skill Behind Extraordinary Relationships.* Autumn Creek Press, 2017.

Tsabary, Shefali. *The Conscious Parent.* Namaste Publishing, 2010.

Van Munching, Philip, Bernie Katz. *Actually, It Is Your Parents' Fault.* St. Martin's Griffin, 2007.

Von Franz, Marie-Louise. *Creation Myths.* Spring Publications, 1975.

Vujicic, Nick. *Stand Strong: You Can Overcome Bullying (and Other Stuff That Keeps You Down)*. Waterbrook, 2015.

Wiseman, Rosalind. *Queen Bees and Wannabes: Helping Your Daughter Survive Cliques, Gossip, Boyfriends, and the New Realities of Girl World*. Three Rivers Press, 2002.

Wiseman, Rosalind, Elisabeth Rapoport. *Queen Bee Moms and King Pin Dads: Dealing with the Difficult Parents in Your Child's Life*. Three Rivers Press, 2007.

Zimbardo, Philip. *The Lucifer Effect*. Random House Trade Paperback, 2008.

Cyberbullying

Aiken, Mary. *The Cyber Effect: An Expert in Cyberpsychology Explains How Technology Is Shaping Our Children, Our Behavior and Our Values—and What We Can Do About It*. Spiegel & Grau, 2017.

Asher, Jay. *Thirteen Reasons Why*. Razorbill Penguin Books, 2011.

Bazelon, Emily. *What Really Happened to Phoebe Prince?* Slate Article: July, 2010.

Carr, Nicolas. *The Shallows: What The Internet Is Doing To Our Brains*. W.W. Norton, 2011.

Hinduja, Sameer, Patchin, J.W. "Cyberbullying Identification, Prevention and Response."

cyberbullying.us. Cyberbullying Research Center, 2014.

Hitchcock, J. A. *Cyber Bullying and The Wild Wild Web: What Everyone Needs to Know.* Rowman & Littlefield, 2016.

Iko, Mizuto. *Hanging Around, Messing Around and Geeking Out: Kids Living and Learning with New media.* The John D. and Catherine T. MacArthur Foundation Series on Digital Media and Learning, MIT Press, 2013.

Lincoln, Ceasar. *Cyber Bullying: The Ultimate Guide for How to Protect You and Your Children From A Cyber Bully (online Bullying, Online Reputation, Bullying Cure, eBully, Cyber Stalking, Bully Free, Abuse).* CreateSpace, 2013.

Lohmann, Raychelle Cassada, Julia V. Taylor, *The Bullying Workbook for Teens: Activities to Help You Deal with Social Aggression and Cyberbullying.* Instant Help, 2013.

McGonigal, Jane. *Reality is Broken.* Penguin, 2011.

Oaksanen, Atte, Matti Nässi, Jaana Minkkinen, Teo Keippi, Marcus Kaakinen, Pekka Räsänen. "Young People Who Access harm-advocating online content: a four-country survey." *cyberpsycholgy.eu.* Volume 10/2: Article 6, June 2, 2016.

Patchin, Justin W., Sameer Hinduja. *Words Wound: Delete Cyberbullying and Make Kindness Go Viral.* Free Spirit Publishing, 2013.

Rheingold, Howard, A. Weeks, (Illustrator). *Net Smart: How To Thrive Online.* MIT Press, Feb.14, 2014.

Rosenbloom, Stephanie. "*Dealing With Digital Cruelty.*" *The New York Times.* News Analysis Article, August 24, 2014.

Turkle, Sherry. *Alone Together.* Basic Books, 2012.

Science and Mind

Allport, Gordon W. *The Nature of PREJUDICE.* Basic Books, 1979.

Arsenault, Louise, Elizabeth Walsh, Kali Trzesniewski, et al. "Bullying Victimization Uniquely Contributes to Adjustment Problems in Young Children: A National Representative Cohort Study." *Pediatrics-American Academy of Pediatrics*: 118 (1) July, 2006:130–138.

Begley, Sharon. "The Brain: How the Brain Rewires Itself." content.time.com July 19, 2007.

Bloom, Howard. *Global Brain: The Evolution of Mass Mind from the Big Bang to the 21st Century* [Paperback]. Wiley, First Edition, 2001.

Clark, Taylor. *Nerve.* Little Brown and Company, March 2011.

Hinduja, Sameer, Patchin, J.W., "Cyberbullying Identification, Prevention and Response." *cyberbullying.us.* Cyberbullying Research Center, 2014.

Kim, Y.S., Leventhal, B. "Bullying and Suicide: A Review." *International Journal of Adolescent Medicine and Health*: 20(2), 2008, p.133–154.

Mlodinow, Leonard. *Subliminal.* Pantheon Books, 2012.

Montgomery, Sy. *The Soul of the Octopus: A Surprising Exploration into the Wonder of Consciousness.* Atria Books, April 5, 2016.

Siegel, Daniel. *Pocket Guide to Interpersonal Neurobiology.* W.W. Norton, 2010.

Williams, Kipling D. "The Pain of Exclusion." *Scientific American Mind*, January 1, 2011.

Zak, Paul. *The Moral Molecule.* Dutton the Penguin Group, 2012.

Web Resources

American Foundation for Suicide Prevention, American Foundation for Suicide Prevention, www.afsp.org. Accessed 3 September 2017.

The BULLY Project, The Bully Project, www.thebullyproject.com. Accessed 23 March 2017.

"Bullying Prevention Resources." *GLSEN*, GLSEN, www.glsen.org/article/bullying-prevention-resources. Accessed 15 October 2017.

Committee for Children, Committee for Children, www.cfchildren.org. Accessed 3 April 2017.

Cyberpsychology: Journal of Psychosocial Research on Cyberspace, Masaryk University, www.cyberpsychology.eu. Accessed 7 July 2017.

"Dark Energy, Dark Matter." *NASA*, NASA, www.science.nasa.gov/astrophysics/focus-areas/what-is-dark-energy. Accessed 23 October 2017.

Empowering Victims, Institute for the Study of Coherence and Emergence, www.empoweringvictims.org. Accessed 19 September 2017.

Graham, Sandra. "Bullying: A Module for Teachers." *American Psychological Association*, American Psychological Association, www.apa.org/education/k12/bullying.aspx. Accessed 18 March 2018.

HelpGuide.org, HELPGUIDEORG INTERNATIONAL, www.helpguide.org. Accessed: 30 August 2017.

High, Brenda. *Bully Police USA*, Bully Police USA, www.bullypolice.org. Accessed 19 November 2017.

"Net Cetera: Chatting with Kids About Being Online." *Net Cetera: Chatting with Kids About Being Online*, Federal Trade Commission, www.consumer.ftc.gov/features/feature-0004-net-cetera-chatting-kids-about-being-online. Accessed 22 July 2017.

Sameer, Hinduja, and Justin Patchin. *Cyberbullying Research Center*, Cyberbullying Research Center, cyberbullying.org. 1 October 2017.

Stop Bullying Now, Stop Bullying Now Foundation, www.stopbullyingnowfoundation.org/main. Accessed 18 December 2017.

StopBullying.gov, U.S. Department of Health and Human Services, www.stopbullying.gov. Accessed 1 December 2017.

"Videos." *Greater Good Magazine*, Greater Good Magazine, www.greatergood.berkeley.edu/video. Accessed 1 February 2017.

"The Web's Most Visited Site about Children's Health." *KidsHealth*, The Nemours Foundation, www.kidshealth.org. Accessed 18 September 2017.science.nasa.gov/astrophysics/focus-areas/what-is-dark-energy/

Films and TV

Bully. Directed by Lee Hirsch. Written by Cynthia Lowen. Produced by Cinereach. Distributed by Weinstein Co. Documentary, April 23, 2011.

South Park. "Ginger Kids." Season 11, Episode 9. Directed by Trey Parker. Written by Trey Parker. Comedy Central, Nov. 9, 2005.

Showtime. "Bang Bang You're Dead." Directed by Guy Ferland. Screenplay by William Mastrosimone. Produced by Norman Stephens, William Mastrosimone, Deborah Gabler. October 13, 2002.

Acknowledgments

I am indebted to my teachers—my very dear patients, students, colleagues, family, and friends.

I would like to particularly thank my very special "bird team" members who, each in her own special way, have been my lifelines through the hardest of times: Bea Harris, Elke Geising, Linda Lewis and Carol LoBianco. And my sincere thanks to my more recent support team members: Janet Roen, Linda and Dave Heinig, Pat Donovan and Maria and Howard Danziger.

Thank you to my first editor, Steffy, who helped me narrow the focus of my writing. And my thanks go to my second editor, Alan Rinzler, who helped narrow the focus of this work even further. And, to Mikel Benton, a truly professional and fearless editor, a big thank you for caring so much about all the things that needed caring about. Peter Cousins, thank you for your patience as I navigated my way through legal and literary weeds. My thanks to Joy Sgobbo for your help with permissions! To Barbara Kim—thank you for appreciating all the forms of my work through the years. And thank you to "eb" for manifesting such an elegant and grace-filled soul through time. Thank you, Barbara G., for inviting me into your "mom's world," which has made my writing time more joyous. And to Alan David, thank you for savoring the finer colors.

And, thank you, Michael Rohani for being the consummate professional in an era when less refined souls roam the publishing world.

I thank my parents for the light of my middle name, which is Hope. It holds in place the given and the chosen.

And to the power vested in me by the Source of all, well, you know how I feel. It's a gratitude that I most fervently try to share with all. I have been true to you and untrue—I'm still trying to get things right.

About the Author

Dr. Becker is a psychologist in private practice, corporate consultant, and was a special education teacher for a number of years. As well, Dr. Becker has been an assistant director and clinician for a division of a private school that specialized in serving emotionally, socially, and academically challenged students. As a guest on professional panels, TV, radio, and quoted in print, Dr. Becker is widely cited as an expert on bullying, children, parenting, and interpersonal relationships. Her Keynote presentations and Workshops are both powerful and fun.

www.ingramcontent.com/pod-product-compliance
Lightning Source LLC
Chambersburg PA
CBHW021408290426
44108CB00010B/432